Competency Mapping & Management
– *A Comprehensive Survey Report*

SUDHIR WARIER

Copyright © 2012 Sudhir Warier

This book contains certain copyrighted contents that represent the intellectual property of the author. It also contains content that are part of a patent application. The author encourages research students to use the material, with prior written permission. Non-commercial usage for furthering research in the area of Human Capital Management/Intellectual Capital Management is also through written request (electronically). For commercial usage please contact the author @ eswarier@gmail.com

All rights reserved.

ISBN: 1502870290
ISBN-13: 978-1502870292

DEDICATION

To my Parents

&

Family

This book is also dedicated to the all the authors whose work has influenced my knowledge in this field

CONTENTS

Preface — i

List of Tables

List of Figures

1. EXECUTIVE SUMMARY — 1
2. ORGANIZATIONAL COMPETENCE MANAGEMENT — 13
3. RESEARCH DESIGN — 21
4. DATA ANALYSIS & INTERPRETATION — 44
5. RESEARCH IMPLICATIONS — 81
6. COMPETENCE MANAGEMENT FRAMEWORK — 102
7. CONTRIBUTIONS TO THEORY, PRACTICE, POLICY & TECHNOLOGY — 133

Key Terms — 151

References — 154

Appendix — 159

Index — 170

About the Author — 174

PREFACE

The rational approach for business enterprises to survive and gain competitive advantage, in the new world order, is through the continuous development of competencies of their employees. Competitive advantage depends on the ability to effectively activate and use organizational resources. This has led organizations to analyze their internal capabilities with a specific focus on employee's competencies. To effectively harness organizations intangible assets a futuristic, dynamic and proactive approach to competency modelling explicitly aligned with strategic business needs and oriented to its success in the long run, is required. Intellectual Capital remains the most unexploited resource within an organization. Knowledge continues to be seen as a static organizational asset. This is especially true for organizations in the Indian subcontinent. The tremendous growth in the different fields of management and research contributions in the last decade has not helped in addressing all the limitations in measurement models.

The modern day organizational landscape is witnessing rapid changes, both in its structure and management. Managing its intangible assets is of paramount importance to an organization irrespective of its size, sector or domain, to enable it withstand the rigors of the current global economies. Only organizations that have a well-defined and integrated Competency Management Framework would be able to successfully survive and compete in the knowledge economies of the future. The major organizational challenges are as listed under:

- The deployment/application of a competency model within an organizational framework including the challenges and best practices
- The customization of models as per organizational requirements
- Measurement of the effectiveness of the deployed model
- Lack of pertinent information on measuring employee

competence

The objective of this research is to evaluate the deployment of competency management frameworks, models and techniques in the Indian industry, identify shortcomings and propose suitable interventions for enhancing organizational competency management initiatives. The primary objectives of this research study are:

- To evaluate the extent of deployment of competency mapping and management techniques in Indian Organizations
- An in-depth study of the deployed frameworks/models/techniques with a view of their identifying shortcomings
- Suggest suitable interventions to mitigate identified shortcomings in the competency mapping and management initiatives of Indian Organizations.

The secondary research objectives include the following:

- To determine the impact of organizational competency mapping and management on its business performance & EVA
- Evaluate appropriate systems, methods and techniques for the efficient application and utilization of organizational competencies.
- To develop a competency model based on the analysis of the data collected through the administration of a structured nonstandard questionnaire

This book, which is unique in its content, structure and presentation, would prove to be an invaluable resource to all 'C' level executives, policy makers, HR managers, Doctoral students, Post graduate and management students.

I sincerely hope that this fledging research becomes the fodder for concrete developments in this field.

LIST OF TABLES

Table 1.1 – Hypotheses Testing Summary 4
Table 1.2 – Pilot Studies Summary 8
Table 1.3 – Data Collection – Sources 11
Table 2.1 - Top Ten HR Challenges 20
Table 3.1 - HR Challenges 28
Table 3.2 – Sample Size Determination 35
Table 3.3 – Data Sources 36
Table 3.4 – State wise Respondent Distribution 37
Table 3.5 – Gender Profile of Respondents 38
Table 3.6 – Age Profile of Respondents 38
Table 3.7 – Respondents Academic Profile 38
Table 3.8 – Respondents Work Profile 39
Table 3.9 – Respondents Employment Profile 39
Table 3.10 – Organizational Size 40
Table 3.11 – Employment Cadre 40
Table 3.12 – Analysis Packages Employed 42
Table 4.1 – Summary – Pilot Studies 46
Table 4.2 – Key Recruitment Parameters 49
Table 4.3 – Cronbach Alpha – Standard Values 52
Table 4.4 – Questionnaire Reliability – Overall 52
Table 4.5 – Internal Reliability of Overall Questionnaire 53
Table 4.6 – Assessment Agreement 55
Table 4.7 – Assessment Agreement – Between Appraisers 55
Table 4.8 - Partial Least Square Regression of Questionnaire Data 57
Table 4.9 – Factor Analysis – Correlation Matrix 59
Table 4.10 – Measure of Sampling Adequacy 60
Table 4.11 – Factor Analysis – Communalities 60
Table 4.12 – Factor Analysis – Component Matrix 61
Table 4.13 – Factor Analysis – Rotated Component Matrix 62
Table 4.14 – Respondents Gender & Age Profile 64
Table 4.15 – Respondents Gender & Work Profile 64
Table 4.16 – Respondents Gender & Industry Profile 65
Table 4.17 – Respondents Age & Work Profile 65
Table 4.18 – Respondents Education & Work Profile 66
Table 4.19 – Respondents Industry & Work Profile 66

Table 4.20 – Organizational Competency Model Deployment 68
Table 4.21 – Use of Standardized Models 69
Table 4.22 – Peer Benchmarking Efforts 69
Table 4.23 – Global Benchmarking Efforts in Indian Organizations 70
Table 4.24 – Impact of CMM on Business Performance 71
Table 4.25 – Impact of CMM on Strategic Capability 71
Table 4.26 – Impact of CMM on Employee Productivity 72
Table 4.27 – Impact of CMM on Employee Turnover 73
Table 4.28 – Impact of CMM on Organizational Agility 73
Table 4.29 – Impact of CMM on Business Innovation 74
Table 4.30 – Impact of CMM on Organizational EVA 75
Table 5.1 – Hypothesis-1 Dimensions 81
Table 5.2 – Hypothesis-1 Testing – Chi-Square Test 82
Table 5.3 – Hypothesis-2 Dimensions 83
Table 5.4 – Hypothesis-2 Testing – Kruskal Wallis Test 83
Table 5.5 – Hypothesis-3 Dimensions 86
Table 5.6 – Hypothesis - 3 Testing - Mann-Whitney 86
Table 5.7 – Hypothesis - 4 Dimensions 87
Table 5.8 – Hypothesis - 4 Testing - Kruskal-Wallis Test 88
Table 5.9 – Secondary Hypotheses Testing 89
Table 5.10 – Hypothesis - 5 Dimensions 93
Table 5.11 – Hypothesis-5 Testing 94
Table 5.12 – Hypothesis - 6 Dimensions 95
Table 5.13 – Hypothesis-6 Testing – Wilcoxon Signed Ranks Test 96
Table 5.14 – Hypothesis - 7 Dimensions 97
Table 5.15 – Hypothesis - 7 Testing – Kruskal Wallis Test 97
Table 5.16 – Hypothesis - 8 Dimensions 99
Table 5.17 – Hypothesis -8 Testing – Mann-Whitney Test 99
Table 6.1 – Research Constructs 105
Table 6.2 – Conceptual Research Framework 106
Table 6.2 – Competency Model for Telcos 115
Table 8.1 - Impact of Standard Competency Models 149

COMPETENCY MAPPING & MANAGEMENT – *A Comprehensive Survey*

LIST OF FIGURES

Figure 1.1 – Research Variables 9
Figure 4.1 – Assessment Agreement – Within Appraisers 54
Figure 5.1 – Deployment of Competency Models in Indian Business Enterprises 84
Figure 5.2 – Commonly Deployed Competency Models in Indian Business Enterprises 85
Figure 6.1 – Research Framework 104
Figure 6.2 – Theoretical Competency Mapping and Management Model 108
Figure 6.3 – Organizational Competence Development Cycle 108
Figure 6.4 – Organizational Competency Management – Key Constituents 110
Figure 6.5 - Developing a Competency Model 113
Figure 7.1– Competency Framework Deployment 143

COMPETENCY MAPPING & MANAGEMENT – *A Comprehensive Survey*

1 EXECUTIVE SUMMARY

1.0 Research Context

The modern day organizational landscape is witnessing rapid changes, both in its structure and management. Managing its intangible assets is of paramount importance to an organization irrespective of its size, sector or domain, to enable it withstand the rigors of the current global economies. Only organizations that have a well-defined and integrated Competency Management Framework would be able to successfully survive and compete in the knowledge economies of the future. The major organizational challenges are as listed under:
    a. The deployment/application of a competency model within an organizational framework including the challenges and best practices
    b. The customization of models as per organizational requirements
    c. Measurement of the effectiveness of the deployed model
    d. Lack of pertinent information on measuring employee competence

2.0 Research Objectives

The objective of this research study is to evaluate the deployment of competency management frameworks, models and techniques in the Indian industry, identify shortcomings and propose suitable interventions for enhancing organizational competency management initiatives. The primary objectives of this research study are:
 a. To evaluate the extent of deployment of competency mapping and management techniques in Indian Organizations
 b. An in-depth study of the deployed frameworks/models/techniques with a view of their identifying shortcomings
 c. Suggest suitable interventions to mitigate identified shortcomings in the competency mapping and management initiatives of Indian Organizations.
 a. The secondary research objectives include the following:
 a. To determine the impact of organizational competency mapping and management on its business performance & EVA
 b. Evaluate appropriate systems, methods and techniques for the efficient application and utilization of organizational competencies.
 c. To develop a competency model based on the analysis of the data collected through the administration of a structured non-standard questionnaire

3.0 Research Questions

 i. *What is the current status of Organizational Competency Mapping and Management in Indian Business Enterprises?*
 ii. *What is the impact of Organizational Competency Mapping and Management initiatives on its key operational parameters?*

4.0 Research Hypothesis

A total of 7 primary and 6 supplementary hypotheses were tested as a part of this research study. They are as listed below:

H1 - Competency Mapping & Management techniques are widely employed in Indian Business Enterprises

H2 - Competency Models are used for selection, training, performance appraisal and career planning by Indian Business Enterprises with deployed Competency Management Frameworks

H3 - Best Practice Benchmarking of organizational competency mapping and management processes along with the use of standard competency models positively impact Business Performance

H4 - Organizational Competency Mapping & Management process strongly impact enterprise economic profits leading to enhanced EVA

- **H4.1** *Organizational Competency Mapping & Management has a positive impact on Business Performance*
- **H4.2** *Organizational Competency Mapping & Management has a positive impact on Strategic Capability*
- **H4.3** *Organizational Competency Mapping & Management has a positive impact on Employee Productivity*
- **H4.4** *Organizational Competency Mapping & Management has a positive impact on Employee Turnover*
- **H4.5** *Organizational Competency Mapping & Management has a positive impact on Agility*
- **H4.6** *Organizational Competency Mapping & Management has a positive impact on Innovation*

H5 - Organizational Competency Mapping & Management has enhanced the ability of Indian Business Enterprises to rapidly and cost effectively adapt to changing business and economic landscape

H6 - Indian Organizations have been able to increase employee engagement and provide superior value proposition (Employee Value Proposition – EVP) by virtue of deploying enterprise Competency Management Framework

H7 - Organizational Competency Mapping & Management calls for substantial investments in terms of time to attain process maturity before realizing significant Return on Investments (ROI)

H8 - Organizational Competency Mapping & Management leads to employee competency development and organizational capability enhancement resulting in enhanced Business Performance, superior Customer Value Proposition (CVP) and high financial leverage

The summary of the hypotheses along with the involved variables, tests employed along with the justification is presented in table 1.1.

Table 1.1 – Hypotheses Testing Summary

Hypothesis	Sub-Part	Description	Variables	Test	Justification
H1	-	Competency Mapping & Management techniques are widely employed in Indian Business Enterprises	3	Chi-Square	Ordinal Data
H2	-	Competency Models are used for selection, training, performance appraisal and career planning by Indian Business Enterprises with deployed Competency Management Frameworks	4	Kruskal Wallis	Non-Parametric Ordinal Data
H3	-	Best Practice Benchmarking of organizational competency mapping and management	4	Kruskal Wallis	Non-Parametric Ordinal Data

		processes along with the use of standard competency models positively impact Business Performance			
H4	-	Organizational Competency Mapping & Management process strongly impact enterprise economic profits leading to enhanced EVA	2	Kruskal Wallis Test	Non-Parametric Ordinal Data
H4	H4.1	Organizational Competency Mapping & Management has a positive impact on Business Performance	2	One Sample Kolmogorov Smirnov Test	Non Directional, Two Tailed test suitable for intermediate sample sizes
H4	H4.2	Organizational Competency Mapping & Management has a positive impact on Strategic Capability	2	One Sample Kolmogorov Smirnov Test	
H4	H4.3	Organizational Competency Mapping & Management has a positive impact on Employee Productivity	2	One Sample Kolmogorov Smirnov Test	
H4	H4.4	Organizational Competency Mapping & Management has	2	One Sample Kolmogorov	

		a positive impact on Employee Turnover		Smirnov Test	
H4	H4.5	Organizational Competency Mapping & Management has a positive impact on Agility	2	One Sample Kolmogorov Smirnov Test	
H4	H4.6	Organizational Competency Mapping & Management has a positive impact on Innovation	2	One Sample Kolmogorov Smirnov Test	
H5	-	Organizational Competency Mapping & Management has enhanced the ability of Indian Business Enterprises to rapidly and cost effectively adapt to changing business and economic landscape	6	Independent Sample Kruskal Wallis	Multiple Independent Groups
H6	-	Indian Organizations have been able to increase employee engagement and provide superior value proposition (Employee Value Proposition – EVP) by virtue of deploying enterprise	5	Wilcoxin Signed Rank	Matched Samples

		Competency Management Framework				
H7	-	Organizational Competency Mapping & Management calls for substantial investments in terms of time to attain process maturity before realizing significant ROI	3	Kruskal Wallis Test	Non-Parametric Ordinal Data	
H8	-	Organizational Competency Mapping & Management leads to employee competency development and organizational capability enhancement resulting in enhanced Business Performance, superior Customer Value Proposition (CVP) and high financial leverage	5	Mann-Whitney Test	Two Independent Samples	

5.0 Pilot Studies

The pilot study for this research work was conducted over 3 phases as outlined in table 1.2:

Table 1.2 – Pilot Studies Summary

Phase	1	2	3
Method	Structured Non-Standard Questionnaire	Structured Non-Standard Questionnaire	Structured Standard/Non-Standard Questionnaire
Questions	19	7	35
Sections	7	3	3
Sample Size	100	150	32
Responses	93	121	31
Valid Responses	82 (88%)	95 (63%)	30 (97%)
Tests	Descriptive Statistics, Missing Value Analysis, Cronbach Alpha, Factor Analysis	Descriptive Statistics, Missing Value Analysis, Cronbach Alpha, Factor Analysis	Descriptive Statistics, Cronbach Alpha, Factor Analysis

6.0 Research Dimensions

The primary dimensions and the elements of this research study are reproduced in the figure 1.1. A total of five dimensions (3 primary and 2 supplementary) are being studied.

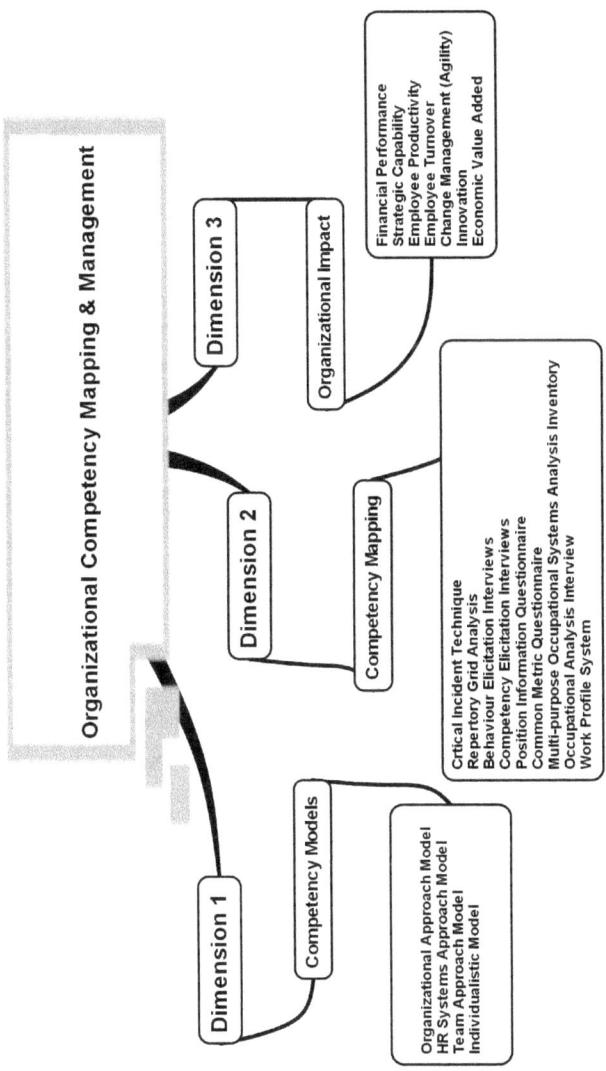

Figure 1.1 – Research Variables

7.0 Research Constructs

The research instrument developed has five constructs and 43 items organized around the 3 major and 2 supplementary dimensions. The broad contours of the data analysis includes determining the current status of the competency mapping and management in the Indian Business Enterprises, evaluation of the benchmarking efforts, gap identification and bringing out specific recommendations to mitigate the gap.

8.0 Sampling Design

A stratified random sampling technique was employed for this study with a view to increase the representativeness of the research study. The aim was to have a significant percentage of respondents from the middle management cadre and junior management cadre. This would ensure that individuals with hands-on deployment exposure on organizational competency management systems along with individuals using CM techniques, tools and systems would be adequately covered. A significant percentage of top management employees were also included in order to ensure management views and strategic perspectives were given due consideration.

9.0 Data Sources

The data for the research study was collected from variety of sources. These includes online surveys, extensive use of social media, traditional paper based surveys and also interviews. The summary is provided in attached table 1.3. A total of 715 responses were received out of which 663 were found usable.

Table 1.3 – Data Collection – Sources

S.No	Collector	Responses	Valid Responses	
			Numbers	%
1	Web Link	161	136	84
2	Email	267	243	91
3	Direct	239	239	100
4	Facebook	39	36	92
5	Twitter	9	9	100
	Total Responses	*715*	*663*	*93*

10.0 Data Analysis

The Data Analysis was classified as follows:
  i. Demographic Analysis
  ii. Status of Competency Mapping and Management in Indian Business Enterprises
  iii. Deployment of Standardized Models and Benchmarking efforts in Indian Business Enterprises
  iv. Analysis of the Competency Mapping & Management techniques employed in Indian Organizations
  v. The impact of Organizational Competency Mapping & Management (CMM) on overall performance

The key research findings were compared with the results of previously conducted international surveys on organizational competency mapping and management. This helped establish issues, best practices and techniques unique to Indian Business Enterprises while validating the conceptual CMM framework

11.0 Key Results and Findings

This research presents a comprehensive status on the Competency Mapping and Management (CMM) activities in Indian Business

Enterprises. It has been able to empirically validate the significant benefits of CMM initiatives. The following is the gist of the key results of this research:

a. The linkage between CMM and Organizational EVA, Human Value Added (HVA), Agility, Strategic Capability and Innovation in the Indian industry has been conclusively established through this research work.
b. This research has also contributed to the development Organizational Competency Mapping and Management frameworks, competency models and has identified the key factors that maximize the impact of CMM initiatives within an organization.
c. The first evidence of linkages between the use of competency frameworks, standardized models, competency mapping techniques, benchmarking initiatives and their impact on EVA, in the Indian Industry has been established.
d. In many organizations, especially in India, CMM initiatives have been launched with much fanfare, but have been subsequently put on a backburner. This study has highlighted that minimum time required to implement organizational CMM initiatives (that bring about some tangible change) is 6 months. Further an additional minimum period of 6 months is required to realize tangible ROI.
e. Additionally in large organizations (with more than 10,000 employees) it would take a minimum period of three years to establish the entire CMM value chain and realizing significant ROI.
f. The work has brought out a set of recommendations for implementing and evaluating Organizational CMM and gathered evidence of their applicability.
g. Lastly this research work has systematically uncovered the key factors that define the success of CMM. It has also helped in designing and validating a functional competency model for the telecom industry.

2 ORGANIZATIONAL COMPETENCE MANAGEMENT

2.0 Introduction

The origins of Competency Management can be traced to the great work "Arthshastra" written by Chanakya, the prime minister of the great Indian emperor Chandragupta Maurya, over 3000 years ago. Arthashastra is considered as one of the greatest work of mankind and encompasses the basics and applications of Management Sciences, Chemistry, Physics, Military and War techniques, Basic Engineering and Technologies, Ethics, Legal and Judiciary and Fiduciary system, Values, Psychology, Anthropology, Organization Behavior and Human Resource Management.

A study has revealed that recruitment & selection based on competencies can shift the performance curve of employees by 10-30% resulting in increased Economic Value Added (EVA) (Hunter, Schmidt and Judiesch, 1990). Further competency based training & development (T&D) and performance management can shift the performance curve of employees positively by an average of 30-60%. The study also revealed that highly productive individuals have a positive impact on the organizational bottom line. Organizations have realized the need for developing and optimally managing their intangible resources to effectively compete in the current day recessionary economies. Thus there is a significant amount of research is being done to develop organizational mapped competencies through the deployment of Competency Mapping/Management (CM) models. Competency analysis is necessary to identify the knowledge, skills and process abilities of individuals to meet the stated organizational goals.

2.1 What is Competence?

The Cambridge Advanced Learner's Dictionary defines competence as "the ability to do something well". The Collins Dictionary defines 'competence' as "Having qualifications required by the work in hand" as well as an 'ability or status' to perform the task in hand. Wikipedia defines competence as "A standardized requirement for an individual to properly perform a specific job". The second and third definitions are apt from an organizational perspective. Competencies can be defined as the cognitive, affective, behavioral and motivational personality or dispositions of an individual enabling him/her to perform well in specific situations. Thus competency can be defined as "The knowledge, skills and attributes (KSA) required by an individual to fulfill his/her organizational obligations. The development of accurate and appropriate competencies results in enhanced organizational learning, performance management while maximizing the usage of the organizational intangible assets.

Emotional intelligence (EI) is a specific set of competencies demonstrating the ability of an individual to manage their actions based on other individual's behaviors, moods, impulses and situations. Studies have shown that individuals high EI are more successful than those who are merely technically qualified.

A modern day simplified definition of Competency would be "The knowledge, skills and attributes (KSA's) required by an individual to meets his/her organizational Key Result Areas (KRA's). Competency Management encompasses all tools, techniques, methods and procedures employed by organizations to assess the available skill sets of its workforce and mapping it in accordance to its current and future requirements. CM involves an organizational need and benefits analysis, competency definition, competency assessment, model building and evaluation as well as model deployment and aims at leveraging the organizational human and Intellectual Capital (IC) to bring about a sustainable competitive advantage and tangible benefits to the organization.

Human capital is the collection of intangible resources that are embedded in the members of the organization. These resources can be of three main types:
  a. Competencies (including skills and know-how)
  b. Attitude (motivation, leadership qualities of the top management)
  c. Intellectual agility (the ability of members to adapt to changing organizational landscape)

2.2 Competency Management - Need & Benefits

In recent years a number of studies have been carried out by psychologists to understand why some people are successful in their careers while others are not. They have investigated the causes for lack of positive correlation between Intellectual Quotient (IQ) and Job performance and tried to arrive at an alternative to the traditional aptitude and intelligent testing that would predict performance. After a number of studies, David McClelland - Professor of Psychology - recognized internationally for his expertise on human motivation and entrepreneurship, arrived at such an alternate variable which he labeled as Competency. Competency can be defined as a reliably measurable, relatively enduring characteristic of an individual which is casually related to and statistically predicts effective or superior performance in a job. The following outcomes of a study by Hunter, Schmidt and Judiesch further bolstered the effectiveness of competency based Human Resources (HR) practices and made the following important conclusions (Hunter, Schmidt and Judiesch, 1990):
  a. Recruitment & Selection based on competencies can shift the performance curve of employees by 10-30% resulting in increased Economic Value Added (EVA).
  b. Competency-based Training & Development (T&D) and Performance Management shift the performance curve of employees positively by an average of 30-60%.
  c. The number of organizations that have adopted competency as the basis to integrate their Human Resources Systems is steadily increasing. A recent study suggests that more than 60% of the Fortune 500 companies have their HR practices based on competency.

d. Explosive growth of the information and communications technology.
e. Increased innovation and reduced cycle times.
f. Deployment of organizational knowledge management systems and effective knowledge sharing techniques.
g. Increased awareness of the importance of organizational Human capital and the associated organizational tangible benefits

2.3   Competency Management - Key Drivers

The changing and highly competitive knowledge economy has made organizations realize that their financial assets represent only a small share of total corporate assets. The most important assets are now in the form of corporate knowledge. Knowledge capital can now be calculated and forms the most important contributory influence in explaining how a firm earns its profits. The success of an organization in the future knowledge age would depend upon the effectiveness with which its knowledge capital is put to use. The following are some of the important drivers for organizational competency management initiatives:

a. Recent studies have established that organizations actively engaged in managing their IC outperform others organizations in the same sector
b. Knowledge Management (KM) is recognized as a core competency that organizations need to develop in order to compete successfully in today's global marketplace. KM is crucial to the adaptation and survival of organizations in the face of continuous environmental changes. The activities of knowledge acquisition, storage and distribution in a KM system enable the dynamic creation and maintenance of an enterprise's intelligence. According to the study about 80 percent of companies look to KM to play a significant role in improving competitive advantage, and consider knowledge as a strategic asset in business. KM involves a thorough, systematic approach to information repository of an organization by a sequence of collaborative processes
c. The new world of business imposes the need for variety

and complexity of interpretations of information outputs generated by computer systems. Such variety is necessary for deciphering the multiple worldviews of the uncertain and unpredictable future. Strategies for surviving in the new world of business cannot be 'predicted' based on a 'static' picture of information residing in the company's databases or individual mindsets. Rather, such strategies will depend upon developing interpretive flexibility based upon diverse and multiple interpretations of the future

2.4 Organizational Competency Management –Key Challenges

The rapid technological advances in all spheres of our life coupled with the ever changing political and economic landscape has brought about a drastic change in the organization, functioning and management of business enterprises. The emergence of the global knowledge economies has brought about an intense competition among business enterprises forcing them to step out from their traditional confines and bring about innovative changes in their operational setup. The primary challenges faced by organizations in their quest to manage their human capital are listed below:

i. Business enterprises have to be highly innovative and agile in embracing new concepts, user preferences and the highly fluid technological advances while coming out with innovative and cost effective products and services to sustain their existence.

ii. In responding to the changes in the business landscape, organizations have become flexible, responsive to the ever changing needs of the customer, cost conscious, environment friendly while adopting a flatter and leaner organizational structure. In the process organizations have distanced from their most prized asset – The employee. However business enterprises soon realized that in continuously volatile economic & technology environment the only way to survive and gain competitive advantages is through the continuous development of competencies of their employees.

iii. Competitive advantage depends on the ability to effectively activate and use organizational resources. This has led organizations to analyze their internal capabilities with a specific focus on employees' competencies. This necessitates calls for a futuristic, dynamic and proactive approach to competency modeling explicitly aligned with strategic business needs and oriented to its success in the long run.

iii. Competency Management (CM) activities are complex to understand as well as implement primarily due to the fact that competencies are confusing and needs to be viewed from the people/employee perspective. Organizations need to understand their core competency requirements on the technical as well as the personal (behavioral) front, identify the behaviors of their best performers and finally duplicate them to drive higher productivity at all levels of the organization.

iv. Another important aspect is that competency descriptions are not uniformly specified nor defined across at the national/international, sectoral or organizational levels. This leads to an opaque competency description market with a multitude of competency frameworks and competency benchmarks. Thus there would not be any uniformity in competency definitions among peer organizations of the member countries within the European Union (EU) or the United States of America (USA). This also implies that there are no standardized ontologies for CM. An ontology in computer science is a formalized description of a domain usually described in a description logics language where the individuals of a domain together with all the classes and their attribute and interrelations between individuals, classes and attributes are defined. This allows automated reasoning engines to be built which by utilizing the interrelations between entities can make "intelligent" choices in different situations within the domain. As a result automated tools such as skill gap analysis, training need analysis (TNA), job search and

v.   recruitment based on individual semantically specified competency descriptions cannot be developed. The major problem with defining a common ontology for competencies is that there are so many viewpoints of competencies and competency frameworks.

v.   A comprehensive research undertaken by Bersin & Associates covering over 700 global corporations have identified the following eight challenges in organizational talent management (Bersin & Associates, 2008):
    a. Workforce Planning
    b. Performance Management
    c. Competency Management
    d. Leadership Development
    e. Succession Planning
    f. Learning and Development
    g. Compensation
    h. Talent Management Software Systems

vi.   Another survey of over 200 senior Human Resource (HR) professionals from private and public enterprises representing 5% of the total workforce in the United Kingdom (UK) have come out with the top ten challenges facing HR resource teams and validate the results of the previously listed work. They are as listed in the table 2.1:

Table 2.1 - Top Ten HR Challenges

S.N	Parameter	Respondents
1	Developing high-performing teams	66%
2	Succession planning	55%
3	Managing talent through change	54%
4	Finding/sourcing talent externally	51%
5	Developing high potential	48%
6	Managing performance	46%
7	Engaging people	44%
8	Assessing best talent to join organization	43%
9	Identifying high potential	43%
10	Selecting best for internal moves	42%

3 RESEARCH DESIGN

3.0 Introduction

There are numerous approaches that can be selected by researchers for finding pertinent answers or solutions to their research questions. There are numerous approaches, put forth by eminent researchers, based on the type and objectives of the research being undertaken. On the basis of an extensive study of the work of these eminent personalities the following are the four main approaches to research:

i. **Quantitative Research**
Quantitative research is generally associated with the positivist/post positivist paradigm. It usually involves collecting and converting data into numerical form so that statistical calculations can be made and conclusions drawn.

ii. **Qualitative Research**
Qualitative research is the approach usually associated with the social constructivist paradigm which emphasizes the socially constructed nature of reality. It involves recording, analyzing and attempting to uncover the deeper meaning and significance of human behavior and experience, including contradictory beliefs, behaviors and emotions. The objective of this research is to gain a rich and complex understanding of people's experience, and not in obtaining information, which can be generalized

to other larger groups.

iii. **Pragmatic Approach**
The pragmatic approach to research involves using the method which appears best suited to the research problem as opposed to choosing one of the conventional approaches. Pragmatic researchers have the freedom to use any of the methods, techniques and procedures typically associated with quantitative or qualitative research. It is evident that every method has its limitations and that the different approaches can be complementary.

iv. **Advocacy/Participatory Approach**
The advocacy/participatory approach is used to address the unique needs or situation of people from marginalized or vulnerable groups. They aim to bring about positive change in the lives of the research subjects and hence this research approach is also described as emancipatory. The researchers adopting this approach are likely to have a political agenda and strive to provide the groups they are studying a voice. The aim of the research is to directly or indirectly result in some kind of reform. It is therefore important to involve the group being studied in the research, preferably at all stages in order to prevent their marginalization.

3.1 Research Methodology

This research adopted a pragmatic approach to finding the answers to the research question. The pragmatic approach is a mixed method that combines the advantages and disadvantages of the qualitative and quantitative approaches while providing the requisite flexibility to handle complex research topics.

Approach
The research employed face-to-face interviews with individuals from across the industry spectrum in order to ascertain the basic details on organizational competency mapping and management. Based on these inputs a pilot questionnaire was prepared and administered to a small group to test its validity. A second questionnaire was prepared and administered to a focus group to

determine additional parameters related to competency mapping and management. Based on the details garnered a final questionnaire was designed and tested for reliability and validity. The data was administered using a variety of techniques including online survey and extensive use of social networking in order to increase the reach, quality and variety of the Reponses. A focused group was created on Linked In, comprising of 453 members – National & International, with the purpose of creating a sounding board, facilitating extensive brain storming, receiving valid inputs and knowledge on organizational competency mapping and management methodologies. The group consists of members who have been part of the core team responsible for competency mapping and management initiatives in some of the best international service organizations. The group also serves as a cornerstone for budding researchers looking for guidance on the subject. This group has been able to contribute significantly in building a body of knowledge in the field of competency management.

The accuracy of the findings of this research has been validated using data from previous research work in the field of competency management. Most of the previous work in the field is global and not localized to the Indian subcontinent.

The data collected from various sources – primary as well as secondary was cleaned, coded and tabulated in order to facilitate statistical analysis. These included descriptive statistics, cross tabulations, classification and regression analysis (CART), regression, modeling and hypothesis testing. Being able to mix different approaches has the advantages of enabling triangulation. Triangulation is a common feature of mixed methods studies. It involves the use of:

i. Variety of Data Sources (Data Triangulation – Primary & Secondary)
ii. Several Different Researchers (Investigator Triangulation – Range of Past Studies)
iii. Multiple perspectives to interpret the results (Theory Triangulation)
iv. Multiple methods to study a research problem (Methodological Triangulation)

Process

The research is based on several (13) hypotheses. These are based on the primary research question (status of competency mapping and management in Indian Business Enterprises) and include predictions about possible relationships between the deployment of competency management initiatives and Organizational EVA (variables).

Data was collected by using a structured nonstandard questionnaire and statistical analysis performed by employing statistical computer packages. The analysis facilitated the determination of the extent of relationship between the variables under investigation. The analysis facilitated the discovery of complex causal relationships and the determination of the extent of influences of the primary variables on each other.

Type

Research may be very broadly defined as systematic gathering of data and information and its analysis for advancement of knowledge in any subject. Research attempts to find answer intellectual and practical questions through application of systematic methods and can be commonly classified as under:

i. Descriptive Research
ii. Analytical Research
iii. Applied Fundamental Research
iv. Fundamental Research
v. Qualitative Research
vi. Quantitative Research
vii. Conceptual Research
viii. Empirical Research

Descriptive research concentrates on finding facts to ascertain the nature of something as it exists. In contrast analytical research is concerned with determining validity of hypothesis based on analysis of facts collected. Applied research is carried out to find answers to practical problems to be solved and as an aid in decision making in different areas including product design, process design and policy making. Fundamental research is carried out as more to satisfy intellectual curiosity, than with the intention of using the research findings for any immediate practical application. Quantitative research studies such aspects of the research subject which are not quantifiable, and hence not subject to measurement and quantitative analysis. In contrast quantitative research makes substantial use of measurements and quantitative analysis techniques. Conceptual research is involves investigation of thoughts and ideas and developing new ideas or interpreting the old ones based on logical reasoning. In contrast empirical research is based on firm verifiable data collected by either observation of facts under natural condition or obtained through experimentation.

This research is a mixture of the various types mentioned above. The primary objective of this research is to ascertain the extent of competency mapping and management in Indian enterprises. This is a part of descriptive research. This research also lists and validates 13 hypotheses based on the analysis of the data collected. This part confirms to analytical research. The research culminates in the creation of a generic (which is empirically validated) as well a specific competency model tailored to meet the requirements of Indian telecom enterprises. This part of the research can be thought of as conceptual research.

Scope

This research is confined to Indian organizations operating within the subcontinent. Although the survey included overseas respondents there were not included in the primary study.

3.2 Research Problem

The rapid technological advances in all spheres of our life coupled with the ever changing political and economic landscape has brought about a drastic change in the organization, functioning and management of business enterprises. The emergence of the global knowledge economies has brought about an intense competition among business enterprises forcing them to step out from their traditional confines and bring about innovative changes in their operational setup. The primary drivers of this research study are as listed below:
   i. Business enterprises have to be highly innovative and agile in embracing new concepts, user preferences and the highly fluid technological advances while coming out with innovative and cost effective products and services to sustain their existence.
   ii. In responding to the changes in the business landscape,

organizations have become flexible, responsive to the ever changing needs of the customer, cost conscious, environment friendly while adopting a flatter and leaner organizational structure. In the process organizations have distanced from their most prized asset – The employee. However business enterprises soon realized that in continuously volatile economic & technology environment the only way to survive and gain competitive advantages is through the continuous development of competencies of their employees. Competitive advantage depends on the ability to effectively activate and use organizational resources. This has led organizations to analyze their internal capabilities with a specific focus on employees' competencies. This necessitates calls for a futuristic, dynamic and proactive approach to competency modeling explicitly aligned with strategic business needs and oriented to its success in the long run.

iii. Competency Management (CM) activities are complex to understand as well as implement primarily due to the fact that competencies are confusing and needs to be viewed from the people/employee perspective. Organizations need to understand their core competency requirements on the technical as well as the personal (behavioral) front, identify the behaviors of their best performers and finally duplicate them to drive higher productivity at all levels of the organization.

iv. Another important aspect is that competency descriptions are not uniformly specified nor defined across at the national/international, sectoral or organizational levels. This leads to an opaque competency description market with a multitude of competency frameworks and competency benchmarks. Thus there would not be any uniformity in competency definitions among peer organizations of the member countries within the European Union (EU) or the United States of America (USA). This also implies that there are no standardized ontologies for CM. An ontology in computer science is a formalized description of a domain usually described in a description logics language where the individuals of a domain together with all the classes and their attribute and interrelations between individuals, classes and attributes are defined. This allows automated reasoning engines to be built which by utilizing the interrelations between entities can make "intelligent" choices in different situations within the domain. As a result automated tools such as skill gap analysis, training need analysis (TNA), job search and recruitment based on individual semantically specified competency descriptions cannot be developed. The major problem with defining a common ontology for competencies is that there are so many viewpoints of competencies and competency frameworks.

v. A comprehensive research undertaken covering over 700 global corporations have identified the following eight challenges in organizational talent management (Bersin & Associates, 2008):
   a. *Workforce planning*
   b. *Performance management*
   c. *Competency management*
   d. *Leadership development*
   e. *Succession planning*
   f. *Learning and development*
   g. *Compensation*
   h. *Talent Management Software Systems*

Another survey of over 200 senior Human Resource (HR) professionals from private and public enterprises representing 5% of the total workforce in the United Kingdom (UK) have come out with the top ten challenges facing HR resource teams and validate the results of the previously listed work. They are as listed in the Table 3.1:

Table 3.1 - Top Ten HR Challenges

S.N	Parameter	Respondents %
1	Developing high-performing teams	66
2	Succession planning	55
3	Managing talent through change	54
4	Finding/sourcing talent externally	51
5	Developing high potential	48
6	Managing performance	46
7	Engaging people	44
8	Assessing best talent to join organization	43
9	Identifying high potential	43
10	Selecting best for internal moves	42

The Indian Context

In India, leadership is a complex change management process. The industry czars realize that the growth of the country depends on effective and sustainable leadership in the business community. Further, in India, the climate for effective leadership is now futuristic in the sense that the focus on the past has moved to a focus on the future. At the same time, there is a mix of tradition combined with technology, new cultural and workplace values taking the place. Paradigm changes for sustainable leadership include:

1. Higher Risk Propensity
2. Innovation
3. Learning & Adaptability
4. Short-term to Long-term Commitment.

A research study has uncovered that those Indian companies that compete globally must have the ability to successfully benchmark against world-class organizations. For them, their challenges include managing sustainable growth, hyper-competition for markets and people, high employee expectations, emphasis on customer relationships and altering traditional company organizational structures. The study identified the following top 10 business leadership challenges of Indian CEOs:
    a. *Consistent execution of strategy*
    b. *Stimulating innovation*
    c. *Corporate reputation*
    d. *Expansion in India*
    e. *Speed &Flexibility*
    f. *Adaptability to change*
    g. *Profit growth*
    h. *Sustained and steady top-line growth*
    i. *Business risk management*
    j. *Changing technologies*

The wide-spread globalization of markets over recent years has resulted in Indian businesses gradually acquiring the characteristics of an industry wherein knowledge is a significant factor in the delivery of goods and services to markets. Consequently, the development and enhancement of competencies amongst employees have come to be regarded as critical for creating effective strategies and practices to enable the continued success and competitiveness of Indian organizations. However Indian companies have traditionally been lagging their western counterparts in adopting organizational level initiatives, more specifically in the areas of Knowledge Management and Competency Management. Over 70% of the Fortune 500 companies have a mature framework for harnessing their organizational intangible assets. However only a handful of the top Indian organizations have such a framework deployed. Further these organizations do not have a holistic enterprise wide framework, but only have certain departments or SBU's has formalized systems for intangible assets measurement & management. The only top organization with an enterprise wide Intangible Assets Measurement and Management system is Infosys technologies.

Challenges

The modern day organizational landscape is witnessing rapid changes, both in its structure and management. Managing its intangible assets is of paramount importance to an organization irrespective of its size, sector or domain, to enable it withstand the rigors of the current global economies. Only organizations that have a well-defined and integrated Competency Management Framework would be able to successfully survive and compete in the knowledge economies of the future. The major organizational challenges are as listed under:

   a. The deployment/application of a competency model within an organizational framework including the challenges and best practices
   b. The customization of models as per organizational requirements
   c. Measurement of the effectiveness of the deployed model
   d. Lack of pertinent information on measuring employee competence
   e. Integration of a competency model with organizational processes and support functions.

3.3 Research Objectives

The objective of this research study is to evaluate the deployment of competency management frameworks, models and techniques in the Indian industry, identify shortcomings and propose suitable interventions for enhancing organizational competency management initiatives. The primary objectives of this research study are:

   a. To evaluate the extent of deployment of competency mapping and management techniques in Indian Organizations
   b. An in-depth study of the deployed frameworks/models/techniques with a view of their identifying shortcomings
   c. Suggest suitable interventions to mitigate identified shortcomings in the competency mapping and management initiatives of Indian Organizations.

The secondary research objectives include the following:

   a. To determine the impact of organizational competency

mapping and management on its business performance & EVA
b. Evaluate appropriate systems, methods and techniques for the efficient application and utilization of organizational competencies.
c. To develop a competency model based on the analysis of the data collected through the administration of a structured nonstandard questionnaire

3.4 Research Questions

i. *What is the current status of Organizational Competency Mapping and Management in Indian Business Enterprises?*
ii. *What is the impact of Organizational Competency Mapping and Management initiatives on its key operational parameters?*

3.5 Research Hypothesis

A total of 7 primary and 6 supplementary hypotheses were tested as a part of this research study. They are as listed below:

H1 Competency Mapping & Management techniques are widely employed in Indian Business Enterprises

H2 Competency Models are used for selection, training, performance appraisal and career planning by Indian Business Enterprises with deployed Competency Management Frameworks

H3 Best Practice Benchmarking of organizational competency mapping and management processes along with the use of standard competency models positively impact Business Performance

H4 Organizational Competency Mapping & Management process strongly impact enterprise economic profits leading to enhanced EVA

H4.1 Organizational Competency Mapping & Management has a positive impact on Business Performance

H4.2 Organizational Competency Mapping & Management has a positive impact on Strategic Capability

H4.3 Organizational Competency Mapping & Management

has a positive impact on Employee Productivity

H4.4 Organizational Competency Mapping & Management has a positive impact on Employee Turnover

H4.5 Organizational Competency Mapping & Management has a positive impact on Agility

H4.6 Organizational Competency Mapping & Management has a positive impact on Innovation

H5 Organizational Competency Mapping & Management has enhanced the ability of Indian Business Enterprises to rapidly and cost effectively adapt to changing business and economic landscape

H6 Indian Organizations have been able to increase employee engagement and provide superior value proposition (Employee Value Proposition – EVP) by virtue of deploying enterprise Competency Management Framework

H7 Organizational Competency Mapping & Management calls for substantial investments in terms of time to attain process maturity before realizing significant Return on Investments (ROI)

H8 Organizational Competency Mapping & Management leads to employee competency development and organizational capability enhancement resulting in enhanced Business Performance, superior Customer Value Proposition (CVP) and high financial leverage

The summary of the hypotheses along with the involved variables, tests employed along with the justification is presented in table 1.1.

3.6 Pilot Studies

The pilot study for this research work was conducted over 3 phases as outlined in the table 1.2.

3.7 Research Dimensions

The primary dimensions and the elements of this research study are reproduced in the figure 1.1. A total of five dimensions (3 primary and 2 supplementary) were studied.

3.8 Research Constructs

The research instrument developed has five constructs and 43 items organized around the 3 major and 2 supplementary dimensions illustrated in figure 1.1. The data analysis and interpretation involved determining the current status of the competency mapping and management in the Indian Business Enterprises, evaluation of the benchmarking efforts, gap identification and bringing out specific recommendations to mitigate the gap.

3.9 Sampling Design

A stratified random sampling technique was employed for this study with a view to increase the representativeness of the research study. The aim was to have a significant percentage of respondents from the middle management cadre and junior management cadre. This would ensure that individuals with hands-on deployment exposure on organizational competency management systems along with individuals using CM techniques, tools and systems would be adequately covered. A significant percentage of top management employees were also included in order to ensure management views and strategic perspectives were given due consideration.

Sample Size Estimation
A common goal of a research survey is to collect data representative of a population. The researcher uses information gathered from the survey to generalize findings from a drawn sample back to a population, within the limits of random error. However, when critiquing business education research, Wunsch (1986) stated that "two of the most consistent flaws included disregard for sampling error when determining sample size and disregard for response and non-response bias". Within a quantitative survey design, determining sample size and dealing with non-response bias is essential. "One of the real advantages of quantitative methods is their ability to use smaller groups of people to make inferences about larger groups that would be prohibitively expensive to study" (Holton & Burnett, 1997).

Cochran's (1977) formula uses two key factors:

i. The risk the researcher is willing to accept in the study, commonly called the margin of error, or the error the researcher is willing to accept.
ii. The alpha level, the level of acceptable risk the researcher is willing to accept that the true margin of error exceeds the acceptable margin of error; i.e., the probability that differences revealed by statistical analyses really do not exist; also known as Type I error.

The alpha level used in determining sample size in most educational research studies is either .05 or .01 (Ary, Jacobs, & Razavieh, 1996). In Cochran's formula, the alpha level is incorporated into the formula by utilizing the t-value for the alpha level selected. The general rule relative to acceptable margins of error in educational and social research is as follows: For categorical data, 5% margin of error is acceptable, and, for continuous data, 3% margin of error is acceptable (Krejcie & Morgan, 1970).

A critical component of sample size formulas is the estimation of variance in the primary variables of interest in the study. The researcher does not have direct control over variance and must incorporate variance estimates into research design.

Cochran (1977) listed four ways of estimating population variances for sample size determinations:
i. Take the sample in two steps, and use the results of the first step to determine how many additional responses are needed to attain an appropriate sample size based on the variance observed in the first step data
ii. Use pilot study results
iii. Use data from previous studies of the same or a similar population
iv. Estimate or guess the structure of the population assisted by some logical mathematical results.

The first three ways are logical and produce valid estimates of variance; therefore, they do not need to be discussed further. However, in many educational and social research studies, it is not feasible to use any of the first three ways and the researcher must estimate variance using the fourth method.

A researcher typically needs to estimate the variance of scaled and categorical variables. To estimate the variance of a scaled variable, one must determine the inclusive range of the scale, and then divide by the number of standard deviations that would include all possible values in the range, and then square this number.

The table 3.2 presents the recommended sample sizes for continuous as well as categorical data based on the work of James E. Bartlett, Joe W. Kotrlik, Chadwick C. Higgins. The candidates for this research work were basically employees in the middle, senior and top management cadres, with some exceptions. The entire population (based on the organizational coverage) is nearly 10,000. The research instrument responses were pre-dominantly based on 5 point likert scale data that is ordinal in nature. It can be thus inferred from the table that the recommended sample size is 623. The total responses received were 715 out of which the usable responses were 663. The sample size can thus be deemed adequate.

Table 3.2 – Sample Size Determination

Population size	Sample Size					
	Continuous data (margin of error=.03)			Categorical data (margin of error=.05)		
	alpha =.10 t=1.65	alpha =.05 t=1.96	alpha =.01 t=2.58	p=.50 t=1.65	p=.50 t=1.96	p=.50 t=2.58
100	46	55	68	74	80	87
200	59	75	102	116	132	154
300	65	85	123	143	169	207
400	69	92	137	162	196	250
500	72	96	147	176	218	286
600	73	100	155	187	235	316
700	75	102	161	196	249	341

800	76	104	166	203	260	363
900	76	105	170	209	270	382
1,000	77	106	173	213	278	399
1,500	79	110	183	230	306	461
2,000	83	112	189	239	323	499
4,000	83	119	198	254	351	570
6,000	83	119	209	259	362	598
8,000	83	119	209	262	367	613
10,000	83	119	209	264	370	623

3.10 Data Sources

The data for the research study was collected from variety of sources. The summary is provided in table 3.3. A total of 715 responses were received out of which 663 were found usable.

Table 3.3 – Data Sources

S.No	Collector	Responses	Valid Responses	
			Numbers	%
1	Web Link	161	136	84
2	Email	267	243	91
3	Direct	239	239	100
4	Facebook	39	36	92
5	Twitter	9	9	100
Total Responses		*715*	*663*	*93*

A focused group was created on LinkedIn, comprising of over 1100 members – National & International, with the purpose of creating a sounding board, facilitating extensive brain storming, receiving valid inputs and knowledge on organizational competency mapping and management methodologies. The group consists of members who have been part of the core team responsible for competency mapping and management initiatives in some of the best international service organizations. The group also serves as a cornerstone for budding researchers looking for guidance on the subject. This group has been able to contribute significantly in building a body of knowledge in the field of competency management.

The state wise distribution of the respondents is illustrated in the table 3.4. 31% of the overall respondents were from Maharashtra. 20% of the overall respondents were from Mumbai. The reason being the physical proximity of the researcher.

Table 3.4 – State wise Respondent Distribution

S.N	State	Respondents
1	MH	250
2	NCR	127
3	TN	70
4	WB	56
5	KN	47
6	GJ	40
7	AP	33
8	KL	27
9	MP	20
10	HR	12
11	BH	11
12	JK	8
13	PJ	8
14	UP	5
15	NE	1
	Total	715

3.11 Demographic Profile

The respondent gender profile is presented in table 3.5. Out of a total of 663 valid respondents 400 respondents were males. Of these the predominant age group was 30-39 years, accounting for 59% of the total respondents as indicated in the table 3.6:

Table 3.5 – Gender Profile of Respondents

Gender	Count	%
Female	263	39.7
Male	400	60.3
Total	663	100

Table 3.6 – Age Profile of Respondents

Age Group	Count	%
21-29 years	17	2.6
30-39 years	391	59.0
40-49 years	204	30.8
50-59 years	51	7.7
Total	663	100

59% of the survey respondents were post graduates while over 35% of the respondents were graduates. These results, indicated in table 3.7, were consistent with the sampling design.

Table 3.7 – Respondents Academic Profile

Academic Profile	Frequency	%
Graduate	238	35.9
Post Graduate	391	59.0
M.Phil	17	2.6
Doctoral	17	2.6

Total	663	100

In order to ensure the validity of the findings respondents from different work profiles were chosen. The work profile of the respondents is listed in table 3.8.

Table 3.8 – Respondents Work Profile

Employment Type	Count	%
Consultant	40	6.0
MNC	148	22.3
Private	436	65.8
Self	39	5.9
Total	*663*	*100*

It can be seen that 65% of the respondents were from the private sector since the majority of the competency management and mapping initiatives are localized to this sector. In order to get a global perspective the survey included 22% respondents working with multi-national corporations (MNC) in India. Around 6% respondents were from consulting companies and family held private business enterprises. The respondents were chosen from diverse industries ranging from media houses to service providers. The respondent's employment profile is provided in table 3.9.

Table 3.9 – Respondents Employment Profile

Industry Type	Frequency	Percentage
Advertising & Marketing	17	2.6
Automobiles	17	2.6
Classification Society	17	2.6
Education	38	5.7
Energy	21	3.2
Entertainment	17	2.6
FMCG	21	3.2
Gems & Jewellery	17	2.6
IT	85	12.8

ITES	23	3.5
Management Consultant	16	2.4
Medical	17	2.6
Service	67	10.1
Telecom	290	43.7
Total	*663*	*100*

Over 43% of the respondents were from the telecom industry and 12% from the IT industry. Large Corporations benefit immensely from organizational knowledge management and competency management initiatives. The organizational size is listed in table 3.10.

Table 3.10 – Organizational Size

Organizational Size (No. of Employees)	Frequency	Percent
<100	136	20.5
101-1000	119	17.9
1001-5000	102	15.4
5001-10000	85	12.8
>10001	221	33.3
Total	*663*	*100*

It may be noted that over 56% of the respondents were from organizations with more than 5000 employees. This included 33% respondents from organizations with more than 10000 employees. The employment cadre of the respondents is presented in table 3.11.

Table 3.11 – Employment Cadre

Employment Cadre	Frequency	%
Support Staff	49	7.4
Junior Management	153	23.1
Middle Management	289	43.6
Senior Management	70	10.6
Top Management	86	13.0
Others	16	2.4
Total	*663*	*100.0*

It can be observed that over 43% of the respondents were from the middle management cadre while over 10% and 13% were from the senior and top management cadres respectively.

3.12 Data Analysis

The Data Analysis was classified as follows:
a. Demographic Analysis
b. Status of Competency Mapping and Management in Indian Business Enterprises
c. Deployment of Standardized Models and Benchmarking efforts in Indian Business Enterprises
d. Analysis of the Competency Mapping & Management techniques employed in Indian Organizations
e. The impact of Organizational Competency Mapping & Management (CMM) on overall performance
f. The key research findings were compared with the results of previously conducted international surveys on organizational competency mapping and management. This helped establish issues, best practices and techniques unique to Indian Business Enterprises while validating the conceptual CMM framework.

The analysis is done in seven phases as outlined in the figure 3.1:

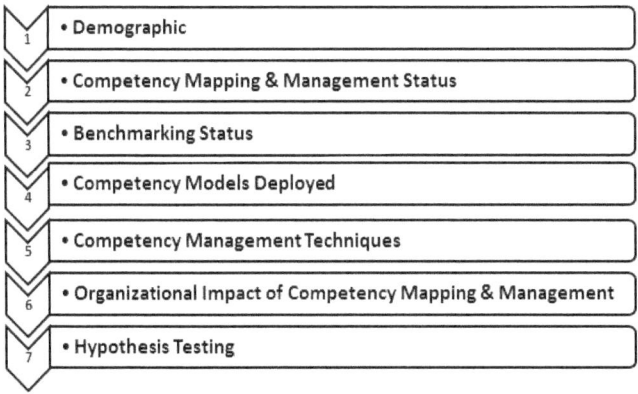

Figure 3.1 – Data Analysis Phases

3.13 Analytical Tools

The software tools employed for data analysis and interpretation are listed in the table 4.15.

Table 3.12 – Analysis Packages Employed

S.N	Package	Version
1	Minitab	14
2	JMP	5.1
3	SPSS	20
4	AMOS	20

3.14 Research Instrument Reliability & Validity

The internal consistency of the research instrument was established by employing the Cronbach's Alpha test. Cronbach's alpha reliability coefficient normally ranges between 0 and 1 with a value of 0.9 or above indicative of excellent internal reliability. The Content validity of the instrument was estimated by critical review by a group of subject matter experts (SMEs).

Factorial validity is important in the context of establishing the validity of latent constructs. Latent constructs, also known as latent variables, are research abstractions that cannot be measured directly. Convergent and Divergent validity are two elements of factorial validity. The Partial Least Squares Regression (PLS) technique is used to establish the factorial validity of the research instrument.

Construct validity refers to the degree to which inferences can legitimately be made from the operationalization in the study to the theoretical constructs on which those operationalization's were based. One can determine of the research instrument is measuring the variables that it purports to by performing factor analysis on the observed scores. The construct validity of the instrument was established by employing Factor Analysis.

3.15 Research Limitations

a. A large portion of the respondents were familiar with organizational competency mapping and management initiatives. 59% of the respondent's organizations had an enterprise competency management framework. Further 70% of the respondents have competency models deployed in their organizations and 69% respondents used competency mapping techniques. 37% of the organizations use standard models. 82% of the respondent organizations had competency management initiatives integrated in their work processes. Further studies should include perspectives of respondents who are on the fringe of adopting organizational CMM initiatives as well as organizations with zero CMM initiatives.
b. The study was based on business enterprises located only in India. 20% of the respondents were from Mumbai. This was due to the physical proximity of the researcher.
c. The percentage of service centric organizations was considerable higher. Other industries including manufacturing should also be accorded equal representation in the survey.
d. This research focused on identifying those measurable human behaviours and deployable organizational CMM initiatives that would help in predicting as well as achieving superior individual and organizational performance. The research did not exclusively focus on the methodologies for developing an organizational competency dictionary.

4 DATA ANALYSIS & INTERPRETATION

4.0 Introduction

Data Analysis refers to the process of inspecting, cleaning, transforming, and modeling the collected data with the goal of highlighting useful information, suggesting conclusions, and supporting decision making. Data analysis has multiple facets and approaches, encompassing diverse techniques various domains including business, science and social sciences. Data Analysis also encompasses the initial analysis also commonly referred to as pilot study. The most important distinction between the initial data analysis phase and the main analysis phase is that during initial data analysis no attempt is made to find answers to the original research question. The initial data analysis phase is guided by the following four objectives: Quality of data, quality of measurements, initial transformations and the validity of the variables to be tested. The figure 1 illustrates the methodology adopted for this research. The main analysis phase is based on either an exploratory or confirmatory approach that is generally decided prior to data collection. This research involves testing several hypotheses and hence adopts the confirmatory approach.

Interpretation of results facilitates in establishing continuity by linking the results of the study with the problem being analyzed while establishing a relationship with the collected data. Interpretation can be defined as the device through which the factors, which seem to explain what has been observed by the researcher in the course of the study, can be better understood. Interpretation enables the researcher to have an in-depth knowledge about the abstract principle behind the analyzed data while providing a theoretical conception which can serve as a guide for the further research work (C William Emory, 1994)

4.1 Pilot Study

The term pilot study refers to feasibility studies which are "small scale version, or trial runs, done in preparation for the major study" (Polit et al., 2001: 467). However, a pilot study can also be the pre-testing or 'trying out' of a particular research instrument (Baker, 1994: 182-3). One of the advantages of conducting a pilot study is that it might give advance warning about the difficulties likely to be encountered during the actual study. A pilot study is especially helpful if there is not much work done previously in the area of the proposed research study. It gives the researcher an opportunity to test and fine tune their research instruments, methodology and design.

Competency Management studies, especially those related to the study of Indian organizations, are very few. Further limited organizations in India are known to have adopted a structured Competency Management Frameworks at the organizational level. A pilot study was thus deemed necessary for establishing a strong foundation for this research. The primary reasons for conducting a pilot survey included the following:

- Developing and testing adequacy of research instruments
- Establishing whether the sampling frame and technique are adequate/effective
- Assessing the scope and extent of organizational competency management activities
- Estimating variability in outcomes to help determining sample size
- Collecting preliminary data
- Assessing the proposed data analysis techniques to uncover potential problems
- Identify potential organizations that could form part of the main study

- Obtain feedback to identify ambiguities and difficult questions
- Discard all unnecessary, difficult or ambiguous questions
- Assess whether each question gives an adequate range of responses
- Establish that replies can be interpreted in terms of the information that is required
- Re-word or re-scale any questions that are not answered as expected

Pilot studies can be based on quantitative and/or qualitative methods and large-scale studies might employ a number of pilot studies before the main survey is conducted. Thus researchers may start with "qualitative data collection and analysis on a relatively unexplored topic, using the results to design a subsequent quantitative phase of the study" (Tashakkori & Teddlie 1998: 47). The pilot study for this research work was conducted over 3 phases as summarized in table 4.1:

Table 4.1 – Summary – Pilot Studies

Phase	Method	Ques.	Sample Size	Responses	
				Total	Valid
1	Structured Non-Standard Questionnaire	19	100	93	82 (88%)
2	Structured Non-Standard Questionnaire	7	150	121	95 (63%)
3	Structured Standard/Non-Standard Questionnaire	35	32	31	30 (97%)

Phase – 1 – Pilot Testing

The first phase of a pilot study involved creating a survey online and sending invitations to a pre-selected sample of 100 people representing the middle and top management cadre. The sample represented a wide spectrum of industries in India. The questionnaire included 19 questions organized under 7 sections. A total of 87 responses were obtained out of which 5 responses were rejected since they were incomplete. The total numbers of usable responses were 82 with a response percentage of 88%. This study was also conducted with the objective of validating the research instrument. The sample selected were individuals who hands-on exposure to some form of organizational competency mapping & management initiatives.

Phase – 2 – Exploratory Analysis

The second phase involved analysis of the data collected. These included descriptive statistics and testing of the reliability of the data. The phase also involved the administration of an additional questionnaire to a selected group of 33 respondents to elicit supplementary details pertaining to the deployment of organizational competency frameworks, competency mapping techniques and their usage within organizations. This group served as an expert panel and helped validate the research instrument.

Phase – 3 – Pilot Testing

The third phase was based on the detailed analysis of the data collected in the second pilot study and culminated in the design of the final questionnaire. 7 questions in the first pilot study were discarded and an additional 12 questions were added in the final questionnaire which had 35 questions organized over 3 sections. The questionnaire employed standardized questions for collecting the demographic information while structured non-standardized questionnaire was used to understand the organizational competency mapping and management processes. The new questionnaire was administered to a 32 participants who were selected using stratified random sampling. These included the 33 participants of the phase 2 study. The data was analyzed to establish the reliability and validity of the research instrument using SPSS Software Ver. 20. The analysis established the reliability and the validity of the questionnaire.

Key Findings

The pilot survey provided major insights to the Organizational Competency Mapping and Management process, especially in the Indian context. The findings, though significant by themselves, are supplementary to the objectives of this research. Subsequent research studies can exclusively focus on the findings of the pilot phase. The pilot studies also helped in establishing the validity of the research instrument. The pilot survey and its subsequent analysis have been accorded a detailed treatment owing importance of the results.

Pilot Survey -1 Analysis

i. The Cronbach's alpha coefficient for the elements of the questionnaire was 0.630. An alpha coefficient value of 0.7 and above is generally considered acceptable. This resulted in the dropping of 7 questions from the questionnaire.

ii. Over 78% of the organizations whose employees were surveyed were MNC's. The respondents of the third survey were therefore chosen so as to include predominantly Indian organizations.

iii. Over 70% of the respondents were from medium and large organizations and 79% of them were from middle or top management.

iv. 50% of the organizations whose employees were part of the survey had some kind of organizational competency initiatives. Only 27% of the organizations to which the respondents belonged had an established CM framework and only 39% of them reported a measurable impact of Competency Management Initiatives on its operational performance. The sampling population was therefore modified in the third pilot study and for the final survey so as to include respondents from organization with a well-defined Competency Mapping & Measurement Framework.

v. Only a small percentage of organizations that were a part of the study had Enterprise wide Competency Dictionaries and employed Competency Elicitation Interviews. The survey questionnaire included only the well-known Competency management techniques. To understand the competency based recruitment process a second pilot study was conducted. In order to widen the scope and understand the competency management and mapping techniques employed

globally the questionnaire was modified and a third pilot study was conducted.
vi. 19% of the respondents were from the telecom industry while 18% were from the IT industry. More than 60% of the respondents were from the service industry.
vii. Only 39% of the organizations included within the pilot survey have mechanisms to evaluate their Competency Management initiatives and only 22% of them have other mechanisms for Intellectual Assets Management in place.

Pilot Survey 2 Analysis

The second pilot survey provided the key evaluation parameters for competency based recruitment and their respective weightages. This survey is unique and the findings can be the basis of a full-fledged research study by itself. The key recruitment factors are presented in their order of ranking in table 4.2:

Table 4.2 – Key Recruitment Parameters

S.N	Key Recruitment Parameters
1	Intellectual Quotient
2	Communication Skills
3	Emotional Quotient
4	Management Skills
5	Technology Skills
6	Core Competencies
7	Behavioural Competencies
8	Academic Profile
9	Relevant Work-experience

Pilot Study 3 Analysis

The pilot 3 questionnaire was designed taking into account the learning's of the previous two pilot surveys. The data was collated and tabulated and tested for internal consistency using Cronbach's Alpha test. Cronbach's alpha reliability coefficient normally ranges between 0 and 1. However, there is actually no lower limit to the coefficient. The closer Cronbach's alpha coefficient is to 1.0 the greater the internal consistency of the items in the scale. A value of 0.9 or above is indicative of excellent internal reliability (George and Mallery, 2003).

When using Likert-type scales it is imperative to calculate and report Cronbach's alpha coefficient for internal consistency reliability for any scales or subscales one may be using (Gliem & Gliem, 2003). The Cronbach's alpha coefficient for the constructs based on Likert Scale is 0.956 which is indicative of excellent reliability.

Data Analysis of Final Questionnaire Data

The primary dimensions and the elements of this research study was illustrated in the figure 1.1. A total of five dimensions (3 primary and 2 supplementary) were studied. The research instrument developed has five constructs and 43 items organized around the 3 major and 2 supplementary dimensions.

The Analysis can be categorized as follows:
 a. Demographic Analysis
 b. Status of Competency Mapping and Management in Indian Business Enterprises
 c. Deployment of Standardized Models and Benchmarking efforts in Indian Business Enterprises
 d. Analysis of the Competency Mapping & Management techniques employed in Indian Organizations
 e. The impact of Organizational Competency Mapping & Management on overall performance

The analysis is done in seven phases as outlined in the figure 3.1.

4.3 Descriptive Statistics

The primary step in data analysis is to obtain a 'feel for the data' collected. Based on this initial feel, detail analyses may be carried out to test the 'goodness of data'. Establishing the goodness of data lends credibility to all subsequent analyses and findings (Uma Sekaran, 2003). The preliminary analyses involve estimating the central tendency and the dispersion. The mean, range, standard deviation, median, mode, quartiles (interval scale data) gives a good estimate of the respondents reaction to the administered research instrument and how good the items and measures are. These preliminary analyses help in detecting any bias that may have crept in. Further a frequency distribution of the nominal variables of interest should be obtained. These may be in the form of visual

displays or charts for easy interpretation. It is always prudent to obtain:
   a. The frequency distributions for the demographic variables
   b. Mean, Standard Deviation, Range and Variance on the dependent and independent variables
   c. Inter-correlation matrix

The examination of the measures of central tendency and the clustering or dispersion of variables gives an indication of how well the questions were framed for tapping the concept. The relevant details are included in the Appendix.

Tests of Normality

It is evident from the descriptive statistics that the data does not follow Gaussian distribution. This was reconfirmed through the Normality test Kolmogorov-Smirnov test & Shapiro-Wilks (Appendix). The value of sig=0.0 is less than 0.05 indicating a non-gaussian distribution.

4.4 Instrument Reliability

A number of measurement models have been proposed to estimate the reliability of a scale (Lord & Novick, 1968). One of the most common reliability estimates is Cronbach's coefficient alpha (1951). However, it has been suggested that Cronbach's coefficient alpha represents the lower bound of the reliability coefficient, because it assumes that all individual items measure the true score of the latent variable equally well (Bollen, 1989; Crocker & Algina, 1986). The coefficient alpha represents a classic model of reliability estimation where an individual's true score is viewed as the average of an infinite number of respondent scores of the same test. Cronbach's alpha will generally increase as the intercorrelations among test items increase, and is thus known as an internal consistency estimate of reliability of test scores. Because intercorrelations among test items are maximized when all items measure the same construct, Cronbach's alpha is widely believed to indirectly indicate the degree to which a set of items measures a single unidimensional latent construct. However, the average intercorrelation among test items is affected by skew just like any other average. Thus, whereas the modal intercorrelation among test items will equal zero when the set of items measures several unrelated latent constructs, the average intercorrelation among test items will be greater than zero in this case. A commonly accepted rule of thumb for describing internal consistency using Cronbach's alpha is presented in table 4.3 (Nunnally, 1978).

Table 4.3 – Cronbach Alpha – Standard Values

Cronbach Alpha	Internal Consistency
$\alpha \geq 0.9$	Excellent
$0.9 > \alpha \geq 0.8$	Good
$0.8 > \alpha \geq 0.7$	Acceptable
$0.7 > \alpha \geq 0.6$	Questionable
$0.6 > \alpha \geq 0.5$	Poor
$0.9 > \alpha$	Unacceptable

The table 4.4 & 4.5 presents the Cronbach's coefficient alpha for the research constructs. It may be observed that the internal reliability of the entire questionnaire as well as individual scales meet the accepted reliability criteria. For demographic profiling a set of standardized questions were employed. These questions meet the generally accepted criteria for reliability and validity.

It may be observed from the table 4.4 that the internal reliability of the research instrument is excellent. Further the removal of any item from the scale does not have any significant impact on the reliability co-efficient as evident from the data.

Table 4.4 – Questionnaire Reliability – Overall

Reliability Statistics		
Cronbach's Alpha	Cronbach's Alpha Based on Standardized Items	N of Items
.910	.910	45

Table 4.5 – Internal Reliability of Overall Questionnaire

S.N	Construct	Variables	Questions	Cronbach Alpha (α)
1	Demographic Profiling	8	Q3, Q5, Q6, Q7, Q8, Q9, Q10, Q11	NA (Standardized Questions)
2	Status of Competency Mapping & Management in Indian Organizations	4	Q12, Q13, Q14, Q24	0.71
3	Competency Mapping & Management Bench Marking Efforts in Indian Organizations	3	Q20, Q22, Q23	0.914
4	Analysis of Competency Mapping & Management in Indian Organizations	21	Q15, Q16, Q17, Q18, Q19, Q21, Q25, Q26, Q33, Q34	0.71
5	Impact of Competency Mapping & Management	7	Q27, Q28, Q29, Q30, Q31, Q32, Q35	0.933
6	Overall	43		0.91

4.5 Instrument Validity

Validity is the most important criteria for determining the quality of a research instrument. The term validity refers to whether or not the test measures what it claims to measure. On a test with high validity the items will be closely linked to the test's intended focus. There are several ways to estimate the validity of a test including content validity, concurrent validity, and predictive validity. Validity was traditionally subdivided into three categories: content, criterion-related, and construct validity (Brown 1996, pp. 231-249).

Content Validity

Content validity is a logical process where connections between the questionnaire items and the constructs are established. Content validity is typically estimated by gathering a group of subject matter experts (SMEs) together to review the test items. Specifically, these SMEs are given the list of constructs specified in the test blueprint, along with the test items intended to be based on each construct. The SMEs are then asked to indicate whether or not they agree that each item is appropriately matched to the content area indicated. Any items that the SMEs identify as being inadequately matched to the test blueprint or flawed in any other way, are either revised or dropped from the test.

In order to test the content validity of the research instrument 5 Subject Matter Experts (SME) in the field of knowledge management and competency mapping and management were identified. They were asked to critically examine the constructs, items in each construct and their relevance to the research being undertaken on a 5 point Likert Scale.

The results were subjected to Attribute Agreement Analysis using Minitab Ver. 14.0 statistical package. The results are pictorially represented in the figure 4.1.

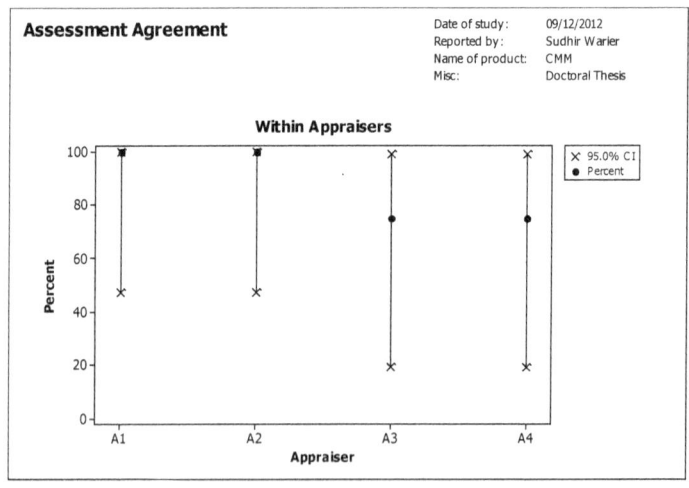

Figure 4.1 – Assessment Agreement – Within Appraisers

The details of the appraiser assessment of the research questionnaire are presented in table 4.6. It may be seen that there is significant degree of repeatability in the assessments.

Table 4.6 – Assessment Agreement

Appraiser	# Inspected	# Matched	Percent	95 % CI
A1	4	4	100.00	(47.29, 100.00)
A2	4	4	100.00	(47.29, 100.00)
A3	4	3	75.00	(19.41, 99.37)
A4	4	3	75.00	(19.41, 99.37)

The Fleiss Kappa statistics for the SME questionnaire evaluations are provided in the table 4.7. Fleiss' Kappa is a statistic for measuring assessment agreement. The values range from -1 to +1. The higher the value of Kappa, the stronger the agreement. If Kappa = 1, then a perfect agreement exists. If Kappa = 0, then agreement is the same as would be expected by chance. The overall Kappa statistics for the four constructs are excellent (Refer Appendix).

The assessment agreement between the appraisers is presented in table 4.7. It can be seen that there is perfect agreement between the SMEs in three of the four constructs. It is important to note that CMM are evolving areas, especially in the Indian Context, and hence there is bound to be some perceptive differences in the evaluation by SMEs.

Table 4.7 – Assessment Agreement – Between Appraisers

# Inspected	# Matched	Percent	95 % CI
4	3	75.00	(19.41, 99.37)

Factorial Validity

Factorial validity is important in the context of establishing the validity of latent constructs. Latent constructs, also known as latent variables, are research abstractions that cannot be measured directly. They include variables such as beliefs and perceptions. While some variables such as gender and age can be measured directly and with little error, a major difficulty arises with surrogates where the abstraction is removed from objective reality. Because such abstractions cannot easily be measured through direct means, agreed-upon practice dictates that they be measured indirectly through several items in a research instrument [Anderson and Gerbing, 1988, Bagozzi, 1977, Campbell and Fiske, 1959, Churchill, 1979].

Each measurement item, i.e., each actual scale item on an instrument, is thus assumed to reflect one and only one latent variable. This property of the scale, having each of its measurement items relate to it better than to any others, is known as uni-dimensionality. Convergent and Divergent validity are two elements of factorial validity. The Partial Least Squares Regression (PLS) technique is used to establish the validity of the research instrument. Unidimensionality cannot be measured with PLS but is assumed to be there a priori [Gefen, 2003, Gerbing and Anderson, 1988]. However, two elements of factorial validity can and must be examined in PLS, as they must be with latent variables in general [Churchill, 1979, Gerbing and Anderson, 1988]. The two elements, convergent validity and discriminant validity, are components of a larger scientific measurement

These two validities capture some of the aspects of the goodness of fit of the measurement model, i.e., how well the measurement items relate to the constructs. When factorial validity is acceptable, it means each measurement item correlates strongly with the one construct it is related to, while correlating weakly or not significantly with all other constructs. Typically, because of the way factorial validity is established in PLS, this pattern of factorial validity is divided into convergent validity and discriminant validity. Convergent validity is shown when each measurement item correlates strongly with its assumed theoretical construct, while discriminant validity is shown when each measurement item correlates weakly with all other constructs except for the one to which it is theoretically associated.

PLS performs a Confirmatory Factor Analysis (CFA). In a CFA, the pattern of loadings of the measurement items on the latent constructs is specified explicitly in the model. Then, the fit of this pre-specified model is examined to determine its convergent and discriminant validities. This factorial validity deals with whether the pattern of loadings of the measurement items corresponds to the theoretically anticipated factors. Convergent validity is shown when each of the measurement items loads with a significant t-value on its latent construct. Typically, the p-value of this t-value should be significant at least at the 0.05 alpha protection level. Discriminant validity is established in the following two instances:

    a. The correlation of the latent variable scores with the measurement items needs to show an appropriate pattern of loadings, one in which the measurement items load highly on their theoretically assigned factor and not highly on other factors.

    b. Establishing discriminant validity in PLS also requires an appropriate AVE (Average Variance Extracted) analysis. In an AVE analysis, we test to see if the square root of every AVE (there is one for each latent construct) is much larger than any correlation among any pair of latent constructs. AVE, which is a test of discriminant validity error attributed to its items. As a rule of thumb, the square root of the AVE of each construct should be much larger than the correlation of the specific construct with any of the other constructs in the model (China, 1998) and should be at least .50 (Fornell and Larcker, 1981).

The data was subjected to PLS and the results are presented in Table 4.8. The analysis was done using JMP Version 5.0 software.

Table 4.8 - Partial Least Square Regression of Questionnaire Data

Variation in CDI				
S.N	X	Cumulative X	Y	Cumulative Y
1	21.5962	21.5961989	89.38834	89.3883429
2	7.294466	28.8906646	8.035245	97.4235876
3	6.278124	35.1687891	1.876896	99.3004839
4	3.379345	38.548134	0.465094	99.7655782
5	3.505928	42.0540624	0.148018	99.9135963
6	5.167004	47.2210665	0.029843	99.9434391

7	2.853119	50.0741854	0.018165	99.9616044
8	3.136532	53.210717	0.011153	99.9727578
9	2.951111	56.1618277	0.00651	99.9792682
10	1.481392	57.6432197	0.00903	99.9882979
11	2.494704	60.1379236	0.002791	99.9910888
12	2.631096	62.7690196	0.001834	99.9929224
13	3.340199	66.1092191	0.001308	99.9942301
14	3.422801	69.5320198	0.001209	99.9954393
15	1.312548	70.8445683	0.002077	99.9975161

CDI or Competency Development Index is the summation of Questions 32, 33, 34,35,36,37 & 39 and is indicative of the organizational benefits from deploying a competency management framework. This is represented as the output 'Y' in table 5.17. 'X' represents the key latent variables from the questionnaire. From the co-relation matrix of the latent factors (not included), it can be seen that each measurement item correlates strongly with the one construct it is related to, while correlating weakly or not significantly with all other constructs. This establishes factorial validity of the research instrument – Convergent & Discriminant Validity.

Construct Validity

Construct validity refers to the degree to which inferences can legitimately be made from the operationalization in the study to the theoretical constructs on which those operationalization were based. One can determine of the research instrument is measuring the variables that it purports to by performing factor analysis on the observed scores. This, in essence, is the definition of construct validation. (Heppner, Kivlighan, and Wampold, 1992) Construct validity was established by performing Factor Analysis. The co-relation matrix of the key construct items is presented in table 4.9. The question numbers of the key constructs are represented by Q_i

Table 4.9 – Factor Analysis – Correlation Matrix

		Q 12	Q 21	Q 14	Q 20	Q 22	Q 23	Q 27	Q 28	Q 29	Q 30	Q 31	Q 32	Q 35
Correlation	Q 12	1.000	.271	.047	.244	.162	.148	-.024	-.024	-.023	.139	.212	.250	.228
	Q 21	.271	1.000	.278	.248	.099	.051	.044	.180	.050	-.028	.109	-.056	.165
	Q 14	.047	.278	1.000	.567	.402	.366	.273	.335	.248	.180	.212	.099	.187
	Q 20	.244	.248	.567	1.000	.756	.686	.595	.670	.577	.451	.630	.591	.746
	Q 22	.162	.099	.402	.756	1.000	.916	.560	.647	.572	.400	.638	.603	.591
	Q 23	.148	.051	.366	.686	.916	1.000	.532	.613	.556	.352	.619	.548	.548
	Q 27	-.024	.044	.273	.595	.560	.532	1.000	.874	.975	.803	.646	.586	.548
	Q 28	-.024	.180	.335	.670	.647	.613	.874	1.000	.844	.702	.758	.494	.588
	Q 29	-.023	.050	.248	.577	.572	.556	.975	.844	1.000	.783	.642	.600	.576
	Q 30	.139	-.028	.180	.451	.400	.352	.803	.702	.783	1.000	.710	.574	.478
	Q 31	.212	.109	.212	.630	.638	.619	.646	.758	.642	.710	1.000	.709	.731
	Q 32	.250	-.056	.099	.591	.603	.548	.586	.494	.600	.574	.709	1.000	.846
	Q 35	.228	.165	.187	.746	.591	.548	.548	.588	.576	.478	.731	.846	1.000

Table 4.10 – KMO and Bartlett's Test - Measure of Sampling Adequacy

Kaiser-Meyer-Olkin Measure of Sampling Adequacy.		.778
Bartlett's Test of Sphericity	Approx. Chi-Square	9833.450
	df	78
	Sig.	.000

The Kaiser-Meyer-Olkin measure of sampling adequacy is 0.778 which is indicative of sufficient factors for each item. The significance (Sig.) is <0.05 indicating that the co-relation matrix is significantly different from an identity matrix, in which correlations between variables are all zero.

Communalities

The table 4.11 presents the communalities. Communalities provide an indication of the amount of variance in the variables that has been accounted for by the extracted factors. It can be seen that all the factors are significant.

Table 4.11 – Factor Analysis – Communalities

	Communalities	
Ques.	Initial	Extraction
Q12	1.000	.757
Q21	1.000	.809
Q14	1.000	.729
Q20	1.000	.839
Q22	1.000	.884
Q23	1.000	.848
Q27	1.000	.937
Q28	1.000	.881
Q29	1.000	.912
Q30	1.000	.828
Q31	1.000	.778
Q32	1.000	.842
Q35	1.000	.773

The table 4.12 highlights the loadings of the thirteen variables on the four factors extracted. The higher the absolute value of the loading, the more the factor contributes to the variable. It can be that the components have significant loadings on the construct items that they are linked to.

Table 4.12 – Factor Analysis – Component Matrix

	Component			
	1	2	3	4
Q12	.186	.545	.580	.298
Q21	.149	.633	-.203	.588
Q14	.405	.468	-.586	-.055
Q20	.835	.349	-.088	-.107
Q22	.817	.237	-.054	-.398
Q23	.776	.210	-.056	-.446
Q27	.859	-.352	-.190	.198
Q28	.875	-.167	-.254	.151
Q29	.858	-.346	-.161	.175
Q30	.751	-.382	.055	.340
Q31	.855	-.047	.201	.064
Q32	.779	-.069	.463	-.123
Q35	.803	.115	.338	-.034

Extraction Method: Principal Component Analysis.
a. 4 components extracted.

The idea of rotation is to reduce the number factors on which the variables under investigation have high loadings. Rotation does not actually change anything but makes the interpretation of the analysis easier. Looking at the table 4.13 we can see that Q27, Q28, Q29 and Q30 are substantially loaded on Factor (Component) 1 while Q22 and Q23 are substantially loaded on Factor 2, Q12 is substantially loaded on Factor 3 and Q21 on Factor 4. All the remaining variables are substantially loaded on Factor 1.

Table 4.13 – Factor Analysis – Rotated Component Matrix

	Component			
	1	2	3	4
Q12	-.063	.078	.843	.192
Q21	.045	-.052	.327	.835
Q14	.078	.510	-.219	.644
Q20	.399	.738	.204	.304
Q22	.319	.878	.084	.063
Q23	.282	.875	.047	.018
Q27	.916	.296	-.074	.070
Q28	.817	.411	-.059	.203
Q29	.901	.310	-.055	.046
Q30	.893	.103	.140	-.026
Q31	.670	.468	.332	-.024
Q32	.526	.519	.461	-.289
Q35	.495	.551	.470	-.052

Extraction Method: Principal Component Analysis.
Rotation Method: Varimax with Kaiser Normalization.
a. Rotation converged in 11 iterations.

4.6   Data Coding & Tabulation

The word 'statistics' has been derived from the Latin word 'status'. In the plural sense it means a set of numerical figures called 'data' obtained by counting, or, measurement. In the singular sense it means collection, classification, presentation, analysis, comparison and meaningful interpretation of 'raw data'. Statistics is defined it as 'the science which deals with the collection, analysis and interpretation of numerical data (Croxton and Cowdon). It can also be defined as "The process of arranging things in groups or classes according to their resemblances and affinities and gives expression to the unity of attributes that may subsist amongst a diversity of individuals" (Connor).

The raw data, collected in real situations and arranged haphazardly, do not give a clear picture. Thus to locate similarities and facilitate analysis data needs to be tabulated and classified. Classification condenses the data by dropping out unnecessary details. It facilitates comparison between different sets of data clearly showing the different points of agreement and disagreement

Data Coding refers to an analytical process in which data, in both quantitative form (such as questionnaires results) and qualitative (such as interview transcripts) are categorized to facilitate analysis. Coding refers to the transformation of data into a form understandable by analytical packages. The classification of information is an important step in preparation of data for computer processing with statistical software. For quantitative analysis, data is coded usually into measured and recorded as nominal or ordinal variables.

Questionnaire data can be pre-coded (process of assigning codes to expected answers on designed questionnaire), field-coded (process of assigning codes as soon as the date flows, usually during fieldwork, post-coded (coding of open questions on completed questionnaires) or office-coded (done after fieldwork).

This research study involved post coding of completed questionnaires. The details of the tabulation and coding are not included for making the book concise.

4.7 Demographic Analysis

A stratified random sampling technique was employed for this study with a view to increase the representativeness of the research study. The aim was to have a significant percentage of respondents from the middle management cadre and junior management cadre. This would ensure that individuals with hands-on deployment exposure on organizational competency management systems along with individuals using CM techniques, tools and systems would be adequately covered. A significant percentage of top management employees were also included in order to ensure management views and strategic perspectives were given due consideration.

The data for the research study was collected from variety of sources. The summary was provided in tables 3.5 to 3.11. A total of 715 responses were received out of which 663 were found usable.

Over 43% of the respondents were from the telecom industry and 12% from the IT industry. The telecom and IT industries are technology and manpower centric industries with a significantly higher churn rate. The rate of technology churn or obsolescence is also very high. As a result these industries are highly conducive to competency mapping and management initiatives.

Large Corporations benefit immensely from organizational knowledge management and competency management initiatives. The organizational profile of the respondents is listed in table 5.34. It may be noted that over 56% of the respondents were form organizations with more than 5000 employees out of which over 33% respondents were from organizations with more than 10000 employees.

It can also be observed that over 43% of the respondents were from the middle management cadre while over 10% and 13% were from the senior and top management cadres respectively. This ensures that the bias is significantly reduced.

The tables 4.14 – 4.19 provide the cross tabulation of the various demographic parameters of the survey respondents. The Questionnaire is included in the appendix.

Table 4.14 – Respondents Gender & Age Profile

Age Group (Years)	Female	Male	Total
21-29	3	14	17
30-39	196	195	391
40-49	58	146	204
50-59	6	45	51
Total	263	400	663

Table 4.15 – Respondents Gender & Work Profile

Work Profile	Female	Male	Total
Support Staff	49	0	49
Junior Management	76	77	153
Middle Management	86	203	289
Senior Management	10	60	70
Top Management	26	60	86
Others	16	0	16
Total	263	400	663

Table 4.16 – Respondents Gender & Industry Profile

Industry	Female	Male	Total
Advertising & Marketing	3	14	17
Automobiles	17	0	17
Classification Society	17	0	17
Education	22	16	38
Energy	1	20	21
Entertainment	2	15	17
FMCG	7	14	21
Gems & Jewellery	1	16	17
IT	12	73	85
ITES	7	16	23
Management Consultant	3	13	16
Medical	17	0	17
Service	46	21	67
Telecom	108	182	290
Total	**263**	**400**	**663**

Table 4.17 – Respondents Age & Work Profile

Age Group (yrs.)	Support Staff	Junior Mgmt.	Middle Mgmt.	Senior Mgmt.	Top Mgmt.	Others	Sum
21-29	0	17	0	0	0	0	17
30-39	49	117	142	34	33	16	391
40-49	0	19	147	3	35	0	204
50-59	0	0	0	33	18	0	51
Total	49	153	289	70	86	16	663

Table 4.18 – Respondents Education & Work Profile

Acad. Profile	Support Staff	Junior Mgmt.	Middle Mgmt.	Senior Mgmt.	Top Mgmt.	Others	Sum
Graduate	32	65	101	3	21	16	238
Post Graduate	17	88	188	34	64	0	391
M.Phil	0	0	0	17	0	0	17
Doctorate	0	0	0	16	1	0	17
Total	49	153	289	70	86	16	663

Table 4.19 – Respondents Industry & Work Profile

Industry	Support Staff	Jr. Mgt.	Middle Mgt.	Sr. Mgt.	Top Mgt.	Oth.	Sum
Advertising & Marketing	0	0	0	16	1	0	17
Automobiles	0	0	13	0	4	0	17
Classification Society	0	0	13	0	4	0	17
Education	0	2	32	0	4	0	38
Energy	0	2	19	0	0	0	21
Entertainment	0	15	0	0	2	0	17
FMCG	0	3	16	0	2	0	21
Gems & Jewellery	0	0	0	0	17	0	17
IT	0	35	28	0	22	0	85
ITES	1	2	17	1	2	0	23
Management Consultant	0	16	0	0	0	0	16
Medical	0	0	0	0	1	16	17
Service	21	20	5	19	2	0	67
Telecom	27	58	146	34	25	0	290
Total	49	153	289	70	86	16	663

4.8 Competency Mapping and Management in Indian Organizations

The primary objective of this section is to evaluate the extent of deployment of competency mapping and management activities in Indian organizations, benchmarking status against peer and global enterprises and the impact of these initiatives on key business parameters.

It may be observed from the figure 5.13 that 59% of the respondents surveyed reported the deployment of Competency Management Frameworks within their organizations. 8 % of the respondents were not clear on the deployment status while 33% respondents reported that there was no CM framework in their organizations. It is however important to note that out of this 33% over 23% had some form of CM initiatives in their respective organizations. The nature of these activities is indicated in the subsequent sections.

Over 72% of the survey respondents reported the use of competency models in their respective work place. The common deployed Competency Models and their subtypes include the following:
1. Organizational Approach Model (OAM)
   a. Normative Model (NOM)
   b. Learning Organizations (LRM)
2. HR System Approach Model (HAM)
   a. Contingency Model (COM)
3. Team Approach Model (TAM)
   a. Campion's Model (CAM)
4. Individualistic Models (INM)
   a. Traditional Pearson-Job Match Model (PJM)
   b. Strategy Based Model (SBM)
   c. Strategy Development Model (SDE)
   d. Intellectual Capital Model (ICM)

The details of the commonly deployed competency models are provided in the table 4.20.

Table 4.20 – Organizational Competency Model Deployment

Competency Model	Count
OAM	246
NONE	203
INM	68
TAM	51
HAM	36
HAM, OAM	29
ALL	16
INM, OAM	14
Grand Total	**663**

OAM is the most widely used model with 206 respondents. This accounts for over 31% of the sample population. Over 31% of the respondents reported that no competency models were used in their organizations. 10% of the respondents had INM deployed in their workplace while 8% used TAM, 6% HAM in their respective organizations. 4% of the respondents had HAM and OAM deployed in their organizations while 2% respondents employed INM and OAM in their respective organizations. It is important to note that 6% of the respondents had all the major models deployed at their workplace.

Use of Standardized Models

The objective is to ascertain whether organizations deploy standardized CM models. It may be observed that over 37.5% of the respondents have reported the use of standardized models in their respective organizations. Of the respondents 40% of the respondents from the top and senior management roles have confirmed the use of standardized models (Table 4.21)

Benchmarking Efforts

Benchmarking is the process of comparing business processes and performance metrics to best practices in the same or across other industries. Benchmarking provides a basis for an organization to compare its systems, processes, performance and financial metrics with its peers in the industry as well as its global competitors (Table 4.22 & 4.23).

The peer CMM benchmarking efforts of Indian organizations are presented in the table 4.22. Only 18% of the respondents have reported peer benchmarking efforts in their respective organizations. Nearly 13% of the respondents have remained neutral in their response.

Table 4.21 – Use of Standardized Models

Response	Support Staff	Junior Mgmt.	Middle Mgmt.	Senior Mgmt.	Top Mgmt.	Others	Sum
NA	0	35	26	32	10	16	119
Strongly Disagree	0	16	15	0	20	0	51
Disagree	16	49	102	4	16	0	187
Neither Agree nor Disagree	0	51	30	17	4	0	102
Agree	33	2	116	17	36	0	204
Total	49	153	289	70	86	16	663

Table 4.22 – Peer Benchmarking Efforts

Response	Support Staff	Junior Mgmt.	Middle Mgmt.	Senior Mgmt.	Top Mgmt.	Others	Total
NA	0	18	26	32	27	16	119
Strongly Disagree	0	1	29	0	21	0	51
Disagree	33	100	132	4	20	0	289
Neither Agree nor Disagree	0	17	43	17	8	0	85
Agree	16	17	59	17	10	0	119
Total	49	153	289	70	86	16	663

Only 4% of the senior and top management have reported peer CMM benchmarking in their organizations. Thus it can be inferred that most of the Indian organizations do not benchmark their CMM activities with their industry peers.

An important point to note is that 23% of the respondents reported that their organizations benchmark their CMM activities with global organizations. A significant chunk of the sampled population – 15% have chosen to remain neutral. The reason for this trend could be the lack of awareness of CMM activities in the Indian industry. The statistics are presented in figure 4.23.

Table 4.23 – Global CMM Benchmarking Efforts in Indian Organizations

Response	Support Staff	Junior Mgmt.	Middle Mgmt.	Senior Mgmt.	Top Mgmt.	Others	Sum
NA	0	18	26	32	27	16	119
Strongly Disagree	0	18	28	1	21	0	68
Disagree	16	50	118	20	17	0	221
Neither Agree nor Disagree	17	34	43	0	8	0	102
Agree	16	33	73	17	13	0	152
Total	49	153	288	70	86	16	662

Another important statistic is that nearly 20% of the respondents reporting who reported global CMM benchmarking in their organizations were from the senior and top management. This is slightly higher (4.5%) that the corresponding figures for peer benchmarking.

Impact of CMM on Business Performance

An important measure of the success of any corporate management program is its impact on business performance. The table 4.24 highlights the impact of CMM on the organizational business.

It can be seen that over 66% of the respondents agree that there is a positive linkage between organizational CMM and its business performance. Over 68% of respondents from the senior and top management endorse the linkage between organizational CMM and Business performance.

Table 4.24 – Impact of CMM on Business Performance

Response	Support Staff	Junior Mgmt.	Middle Mgmt.	Senior Mgmt.	Top Mgmt.	Others	Sum
NA	0	0	13	32	7	16	68
Disagree	0	15	15	0	4	0	34
Neither Agree nor Disagree	16	52	45	0	6	0	119
Agree	33	70	216	38	51	0	408
Strongly Agree	0	16	0	0	18	0	34
Total	49	153	289	70	86	16	663

Impact of CMM on Strategic Capability

The impact of organizational CMM activities on its strategic capability is presented in table 4.25. The strategic capability of an organization indicates the degree of organizations ability to adapt itself to changing social and business environments. 51% of the respondents have endorsed the positive linkage of organizational CMM and its strategic capabilities. This includes over 61% of senior and top management respondents.

Table 4.25 – Impact of CMM on Strategic Capability

Responses	Support Staff	Junior Mgmt.	Middle Mgmt.	Senior Mgmt.	Top Mgmt.	Others	Sum
NA	0	1	26	32	10	16	85
Disagree	0	15	15	0	4	0	34
Neither Agree nor Disagree	33	52	74	1	10	0	170
Agree	16	69	174	37	44	0	340
Strongly Agree	0	16	0	0	18	0	34
Total	49	153	289	70	86	16	663

Impact of CMM on Employee Productivity

In times of challenging socio-economic conditions the measurement and management of employee productivity assumes paramount importance. The challenge lies in enhancing employee productivity by eliminating the non-value activities, processes from the work cycle. This is where organizational CMM initiatives play a major role. Over 64% of the respondents have reported the role of CMM in enhancing employee productivity. It goes with saying that an increase in employee productivity will lead to enhanced business performance and an increase in the strategic capability of the organization in the long run. This view is supported by more than 67% of the respondents from the senior and top management cadre (Table 4.26).

Table 4.26 – Impact of CMM on Employee Productivity

Responses	Support Staff	Junior Mgmt.	Middle Mgmt.	Senior Mgmt.	Top Mgmt.	Others	Sum
NA	0	0	13	32	7	16	68
Disagree	16	15	15	0	5	0	51
Neither Agree nor Disagree	16	36	59	0	8	0	119
Agree	17	86	202	38	65	0	408
Strongly Agree	0	16	0	0	1	0	17
Total	**49**	**153**	**289**	**70**	**86**	**16**	**663**

Impact of CMM on Employee Turnover

Employee Turnover is defined as the ratio of the number of workers that had to be replaced in a given time period to the average number of workers while attrition is the reduction in staff and employees in a company through normal means, such as retirement and resignation. Employee turnover is a huge challenge and a potential impediment in organizational growth and success. Nearly 36% of respondents believe that organizational CMM activities lead to a reduction in ET. This includes 44% of respondents from the senior and top management (Table 4.27)

Table 4.27 – Impact of CMM on Employee Turnover

Response	Support Staff	Junior Mgmt.	Middle Mgmt.	Senior Mgmt.	Top Mgmt.	Others	Sum
NA	0	15	13	32	9	16	85
Strongly Disagree	17	0	0	0	0	0	17
Disagree	0	31	31	0	6	0	68
Neither Agree nor Disagree	32	54	129	19	21	0	255
Agree	0	37	116	19	32	0	204
Strongly Agree	0	16	0	0	18	0	34
Total	49	153	289	70	86	16	663

Impact of CMM on Organizational Agility

Agility, on an organizational level, refers to efficiency with which an organization can respond to change. 38 % of the respondents support the positive linkage between CMM and the ability of the organizations to respond to changes in its offerings to meet changes in external business environment. This view is endorsed by over 55% of the senior and top management respondents as highlighted in the cross tabulation presented in table 4.28.

Table 4.28 – Impact of CMM on Organizational Agility

Response	Support Staff	Junior Mgmt.	Middle Mgmt.	Senior Mgmt.	Top Mgmt.	Others	Sum
NA	0	16	43	32	12	16	119
Strongly Disagree	17	0	0	0	0	0	17
Disagree	16	15	0	0	3	0	34
Neither Agree nor Disagree	0	56	159	3	20	0	238
Agree	16	50	87	18	50	0	221
Strongly Agree	0	16	0	17	1	0	34
Total	49	153	289	70	86	16	663

Impact of CMM on Innovation

Innovation refers to the ability of an organization to ensure its sustenance and competitive advantage through the design and development of innovative product and services in tune with the external socio-economic environment. 41% of the survey respondents believe that organization CMM has contributed to increased innovation within their workplace. This view is supported by 57% of the respondents mapped to the senior and top management cadres, as presented in the table 4.29.

Table 4.29 – Impact of CMM on Business Innovation

Response	Support Staff	Junior Mgmt.	Middle Mgmt.	Senior Mgmt.	Top Mgmt.	Others	Sum
NA	0	50	59	32	13	16	170
Disagree	0	16	29	0	6	0	51
Neither Agree nor Disagree	33	21	100	2	14	0	170
Agree	16	50	101	19	52	0	238
Strongly Agree	0	16	0	17	1	0	34
Total	49	153	289	70	86	16	663

Impact of CMM on Organizational EVA

EVA is a direct financial performance measure of the creation of shareholder wealth over a period of time. A strong EVA is highly desired irrespective of the organizational demographics. A positive impact on EVA is the ultimate endorsement of the efficacy of any management initiative. More than 41% of the respondents believe that there is a strong positive impact of organizational CMM initiatives on its EVA. This view is strongly supported by over 66% of the top and senior management respondents as shown in table 4.30. The top and the senior management employees are the ones that are involved in estimating the EVA of an organization; hence their view point is highly important.

Table 4.30 – Impact of CMM on Organizational EVA

Response	Support Staff	Junior Mgmt.	Middle Mgmt.	Senior Mgmt.	Top Mgmt.	Others	Sum
NA	16	68	72	32	17	16	221
Disagree	0	15	15	0	4	0	34
Neither Agree nor Disagree	0	20	116	3	14	0	153
Agree	33	50	86	35	51	0	255
Total	49	153	289	70	86	16	663

4.9 Co-relational Analysis

A co-relational analysis was done on the primary construct items. The statistical table has been omitted to simplify presentation. The following are the interpretation of the co-relation:

Inferences

There exists a strong co-relation between:
1. Deployment of Competency Management Frameworks and use of competency mapping techniques
2. Use of standard competency models and peer benchmarking initiatives
3. Peer benchmarking and Global benchmarking initiatives
4. Peer benchmarking and Innovation
5. Global benchmarking and Innovation
6. Business performance and Organizational Strategic Capabilities
7. Business performance and Employee Productivity
8. Business performance and Employee Turnover
9. Business performance and Innovation
10. Business performance and EVA
11. Employee productivity and Organizational Strategic Capability
12. Employee Turnover and Organizational Strategic Capability
13. Organizational Strategic Capability and Agility
14. Organizational Strategic Capability and Innovation
15. Organizational Strategic Capability and EVA

16. Employee Productivity and Employee Turnover
17. Employee Productivity and Innovation
18. Employee Productivity and EVA
19. Agility & Innovation
20. Agility and EVA
21. Innovation and EVA

There exists medium co-relation between:
1. Deployment of Competency Management Framework and competency models
2. Deployment of Competency Management Framework and use of standard competency models
3. Use of competency models and competency mapping techniques
4. Use of competency models and organizational competency dictionaries
5. Peer benchmarking initiatives and Organizational Agility
6. Global benchmarking activities and Organizational EVA
7. Use of standard competency models and competency dictionaries
8. Peer benchmarking and timeline for CMM implementation
9. Use of standard competency models and CMM implementation timeline
10. Peer benchmarking initiatives and Employee Turnover
11. Use of competency mapping techniques and Organizational EVA

There exists medium negative co-relation between:
1. Use of competency models and Global Benchmarking initiatives
2. Use of competency models and Peer Benchmarking initiatives
3. Use of competency models and Business Performance
4. Use of competency models and Employee Productivity
5. Use of competency mapping techniques and Global Benchmarking initiatives
6. Use of competency mapping techniques and Organizational EVA
7. Competency Dictionary and Employee Turnover

8. CMM Implementation Timeline and Organizational EVA

The co-relational analysis of the primary construct items with CDI (Competency Deployment Index) was performed and the key findings are as listed:

Inferences
There exists a strong co-relation between:
1. Deployment of Organizational Competency Management Framework and Competency Mapping techniques
2. Use of standardized models and Peer Benchmarking initiatives
3. Global Benchmarking Initiatives and Peer Benchmarking
4. Peer Benchmarking initiatives and Standardized Models
5. Peer Benchmarking initiatives and Organizational EVA

There exists medium co-relation between:
1. Deployment of Organizational Competency Management Framework and use of Competency Models
2. Deployment of Organizational Competency Management Framework and use of Standard Competency Models
3. Deployment of Organizational Competency Management Framework and Peer Benchmarking initiatives
4. Deployment of Organizational Competency Management Framework and use of Organizational Competency Dictionaries
5. Deployment of Organizational Competency Management Framework and CDI
6. Use of Competency Models and deployment of Competency Mapping Techniques
7. Use of Competency Models and deployment of Organizational Competency Dictionaries
8. Use of Competency Models and CDI
9. Use of Competency Mapping Techniques and deployment of Organizational Competency Dictionaries
10. Use of Competency Mapping Techniques and CDI
11. Global Benchmarking initiatives and CDI
12. Use of Standard Competency Models and Global Benchmarking initiatives

13. Use of Standard Competency Models and deployment of Organizational Competency Dictionaries
14. Use of Standard Competency Models and CMM Implementation Timeline
15. Use of Standard Competency Models and CDI
16. Global Benchmarking and Peer Benchmarking initiatives
17. CMM ROI Timeline and CDI

There exists negative co-relation between:
1. Use of Competency Models and Global Benchmarking Efforts
2. Use of Competency Models and Peer Benchmarking Efforts
3. Use of Competency Mapping Techniques and Global Benchmarking efforts

Summary

1. The pilot surveys provided major insights to the Organizational Competency Mapping and Management process, especially in the Indian context.
2. It also provided the key evaluation parameters for competency based recruitment and their respective weightages.
3. This pilot survey 2 can be the basis of a full-fledged research study by itself. Based on the preliminary findings of this survey the researcher has filed a patent application in India.
4. The data analysis was done in seven phases.
5. The research instrument was tested for reliability and validity
6. A stratified random sampling technique was employed for this study with a view to increase the representativeness of the research study.
7. The aim was to have a significant percentage of respondents from the middle management cadre and junior management cadre in order to ensure that individuals with hands-on deployment exposure on organizational competency management systems and techniques would be adequately represented.
8. A significant percentage of top management employees were also included in order to ensure management views and strategic perspectives were given due consideration.

Survey Conclusions

1. The internal reliability of the research instrument was found to be excellent.
2. The instrument was tested for content, criterion-related, and construct validity.
3. 59% of the respondents surveyed reported the deployment of Competency Management Frameworks within their organizations.
4. 33% respondents reported that there was no CM framework in their organizations. It is however to important to note that out of this 33% over 23% had some form of CM initiatives deployed.
5. Over 72% of the survey respondents reported the use of competency models in their respective work place.
6. Organization Approach Model is the most widely used model with 206 respondents. This accounts for over 31% of the sample population.
7. Over 37.5% of the respondents use standardized models in their organizations
8. Only 18% of the respondents have reported peer benchmarking efforts in their respective organizations.
9. However 23% of the respondents reported that their organizations benchmark their CMM activities with global organizations.
10. 66% of the respondents agree that there is a positive linkage between organizational CMM and its business performance.
11. 51% of the respondents have endorsed the positive linkage of organizational CMM and its strategic capabilities. This includes over 61% of senior and top management respondents.
12. 64% of the respondents have reported the role of CMM in enhancing employee productivity. This view is supported by more than 67% of the respondents from the senior and top management cadre.
13. 36% of respondents believe that organizational CMM activities lead to a reduction in Employee Turnover. This includes 44% of respondents from the senior and

top management.
14. 38 % of the respondents support the positive linkage between CMM and the ability of the organizations to respond to changes in its offerings to meet changes in external business environment. This view is endorsed by over 55% of the senior and top management.
15. 41% of the survey respondents believe that organizational Competency Mapping and Management has contributed to increased innovation within their workplaces. This view is supported by 57% of the respondents mapped to the senior and top management cadres.
16. 41% of the respondents believe that there is a strong positive impact of organizational CMM initiatives on its EVA. This view is strongly supported by over 66% of the top and senior management respondents.

5 RESEARCH IMPLICATIONS

5.0 Testing

The constructs, the dimensions and the variables employed for testing the hypothesis is presented in table 5.1.

Table 5.1 – Hypothesis-1 Dimensions

S.N	Construct	Dimension	Q.No
1	Status of Competency Mapping & Management in Indian Organizations	Competency Management Framework Deployment	12
2	Status of Competency Mapping & Management in Indian Organizations	Use of Competency Models	14
3	Status of Competency Mapping & Management in Indian Organizations	Use of Competency Mapping Techniques	24

Null Hypothesis - HO1

HO1 Competency Mapping & Management techniques are not widely employed in Indian Business Enterprises

Testing

From the table 5.2, it can be observed that the value of $p < 0.05$. The null hypothesis is therefore rejected.

Table 5.2 – Hypothesis-1 Testing – Chi-Square Test

	Q12	Q14	Q24
Chi-Square	48.340[a]	130.186[b]	758.026[c]
df	1	1	3
Asymp. Sig.	.000	.000	.000

Research Implication – 1

59% of the respondent's organizations had a competency management framework in place. Further 70% of the respondents have competency models deployed in their organizations (figure 6.2) and 69% respondents used competency mapping techniques. Thus it can be conclusively proven that Competency Mapping & Management techniques are widely employed in Indian Business Enterprises

Null Hypothesis - HO2

HO2 Competency Models are rarely used for selection, training, performance appraisal and career planning by Indian Business Enterprises with deployed Competency Management Frameworks

The constructs, the dimensions and the variables employed for testing the hypothesis is presented in the table 5.3.

Table 5.3 – Hypothesis-2 Dimensions

S.N	Construct	Dimension	Q No.
1	Status of Competency Mapping & Management in Indian Organizations	Competency Management Framework Deployment	12
2	Status of Competency Mapping & Management in Indian Organizations	Use of Competency Models	14
3	Status of Competency Mapping & Management in Indian Organizations	Use of Competency Mapping Techniques	24
4	Competency Mapping & Management Bench Marking Efforts in Indian Organizations	Use of Standardized Competency Models	20

Testing

From the table 5.4, it can be observed that the value of $p < 0.001$. The null hypothesis is therefore rejected.

Table 5.4 – Hypothesis-2 Testing – Kruskal Wallis Test

Test Statistics[a,b]						
Chi-Square			85.789	71.729	254.842	250.401
df			2	2	2	2
Asymp. Sig.			.000	.000	.000	.000
Monte Carlo Sig.	Sig.		.000[c]	.000[c]	.000[c]	.000[c]
	99% Confidence Interval	Lower Bound	.000	.000	.000	.000
		Upper Bound	.007	.007	.007	.007
a. Kruskal Wallis Test						
b. Grouping Variable: Q12						

The frequency distribution of the respondents on the

deployment of competency models in their respective organizations is presented in figure 5.1. It can be inferred from figure that over 70% of the respondents had competency models deployed in their respective work places.

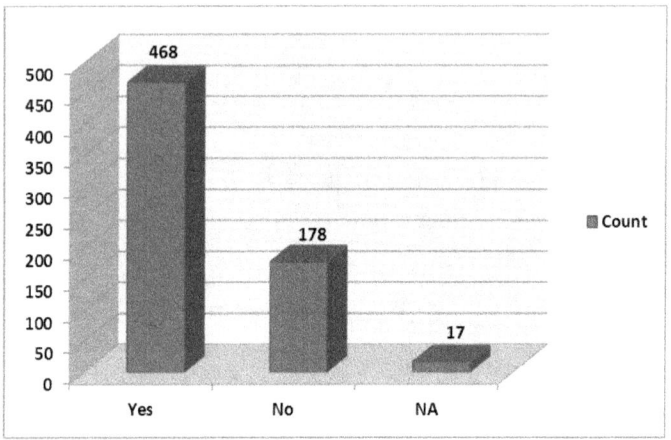

Figure 5.1 – Deployment of Competency Models in Indian Business Enterprises

The type of competency models as provided by the survey respondents are charted in figure 5.2. The most commonly deployed competency model was the Organization Approach Model (65% respondents) followed by Individualistic Models (21% respondents), HR System Approach Model (18% respondents) and Team Approach Model (14% respondents).

Around 4% of the respondents reported that they had all the four models deployed in their respective organizations and 11% of the respondents reported they had Organization Approach Model and HR System Approach Model deployed in their organizations.

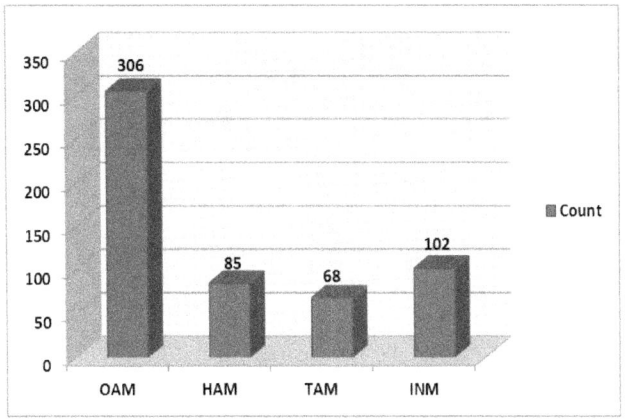

Figure 5.2 – Commonly Deployed Competency Models in Indian Business Enterprises

Research Implication - 2

It is conclusively established that Competency Models are used for selection, training, performance appraisal and career planning by Indian Business Enterprises with deployed Competency Management Frameworks. This leads to enhanced Organizational HRVA (Human Resource Value Added)

HO3 Best Practice Benchmarking of organizational competency mapping and management processes along with the use of standard competency models does not have any positive impact Business Performance

The constructs, the dimensions and the variables employed for testing the hypothesis is presented in table 5.5.

Table 5.5 – Hypothesis-3 Dimensions

S.N	Construct	Dimension	Q No.
1	Competency Mapping & Management Bench Marking Efforts in Indian Organizations	Use of Standardized Competency Models	20
2	Competency Mapping & Management Bench Marking Efforts in Indian Organizations	Benchmarking against Peer Organizations	22
3	Competency Mapping & Management Bench Marking Efforts in Indian Organizations	Benchmarking against Global Enterprises	23
4	Impact of Competency Mapping & Management	Business Performance	27

Testing

From the table 5.6, it can be observed that the value of $p < 0.05$. The null hypothesis stands rejected.

Table 5.6 – Hypothesis - 3 Testing - Mann-Whitney Test

Test Statistics[a,b]			
	Q20	Q22	Q23
Chi-Square	24.798	98.910	41.409
df	2	2	2
Asymp. Sig.	.000	.000	.000
a. Kruskal Wallis Test			
b. Grouping Variable: Q27			

The variables representing Organizational Competency Dictionary Deployment & Impact on Strategic Capability were cross tabulated and their co-relation coefficients determined. There is significant positive co-relation between the use of standard competency models and organizational business performance.

Research Implication - 3

It is conclusively established that Best Practice Benchmarking of organizational competency mapping and management processes along with the use of standard competency models positively impact Business Performance.

HO4 *Organizational Competency Mapping & Management process does not positively impact enterprise economic profits leading to enhanced EVA*

The constructs, the dimensions and the variables employed for testing the hypothesis is presented in table 5.7.

Table 5.7 – Hypothesis - 4 Dimensions

S.N	Construct	Dimension	Q No.
1	Status of Competency Mapping & Management in Indian Organizations	Competency Management Framework Deployment	12
2	Status of Competency Mapping & Management in Indian Organizations	Use of Competency Models	14
3	Status of Competency Mapping & Management in Indian Organizations	Use of Organizational Competency Mapping	24
4	Analysis of Competency Mapping & Management in Indian Organizations	Use of Organizational Competency Dictionary	21
5	Impact of Competency Mapping & Management	Business Performance	27
6	Impact of Competency Mapping & Management	Strategic Capability	28
7	Impact of Competency Mapping & Management	Employee Productivity	29

S.N	Construct	Dimension	Q. No.
8	Impact of Competency Mapping & Management	Employee Turnover	30
9	Impact of Competency Mapping & Management	Agility	31
10	Impact of Competency Mapping & Management	Innovation	32
11	Impact of Competency Mapping & Management	EVA	35

Testing

The results of Kruskal-Wallis test for hypothesis is presented in the table 5.8. It can be observed that the value of $p < 0.05$. This rejects the null hypothesis and accepts the alternative hypothesis.

Table 5.8 – Hypothesis - 4 Testing - Kruskal-Wallis Test

Test Statistics[a,b]	
	Q35
Chi-Square	154.451
df	1
Asymp. Sig.	.000
a. Kruskal Wallis Test	
b. Grouping Variable: Q12	

Secondary Hypotheses

1. *HO4.1*   *Organizational Competency Mapping & Management does not positively impact Business Performance*
2. *HO4.2*   *Organizational Competency Mapping & Management does not positively impact Strategic Capability*
3. *HO4.3*   *Organizational Competency Mapping & Management does not positively impact Employee Productivity*
4. *HO4.4*   *Organizational Competency Mapping & Management does not positively impact Employee Turnover*

5. HO4.5   Organizational Competency Mapping & Management does not positively impact Agility
6. HO4.6   Organizational Competency Mapping & Management does not positively impact Innovation

Secondary Hypothesis Testing

The secondary hypotheses was tested using the One Sample Kolmogorov Smirnov test. The result summary is presented in the table 5.9. The test rejects the secondary null hypotheses.

Table 5.9 – Secondary Hypotheses Testing – One-Sample Kolmogorov Smirnov Test

Hypothesis Test Summary

	Null Hypothesis	Test	Sig.	Decision
1	The distribution of Q27 is normal with mean 3.26 and standard deviation 1.57.	One-Sample Kolmogorov-Smirnov Test	.000	Reject the null hypothesis.
2	The distribution of Q28 is normal with mean 3.05 and standard deviation 1.68.	One-Sample Kolmogorov-Smirnov Test	.000	Reject the null hypothesis.
3	The distribution of Q29 is normal with mean 3.18 and standard deviation 1.55.	One-Sample Kolmogorov-Smirnov Test	.000	Reject the null hypothesis.
4	The distribution of Q30 is normal with mean 2.74 and standard deviation 1.65.	One-Sample Kolmogorov-Smirnov Test	.000	Reject the null hypothesis.
5	The distribution of Q31 is normal with mean 2.62 and standard deviation 1.85.	One-Sample Kolmogorov-Smirnov Test	.000	Reject the null hypothesis.
6	The distribution of Q32 is normal with mean 2.36 and standard deviation 2.08.	One-Sample Kolmogorov-Smirnov Test	.000	Reject the null hypothesis.

Asymptotic significances are displayed. The significance level is .05.

Impact of Organizational Competency Management Framework

The cross tabulation of the use of competency management framework and its impact on organizational Economic Value Added (EVA) was computed. Economic Value Added is an estimate of an organization's economic profit and represents the value created in excess of the required return of the stakeholders (Investopedia , 2011) EVA is a direct financial performance measure of the creation of shareholder wealth over a period of time. A high EVA is highly desirable. It may be observed that over 52% of the respondents in organizations with competency management framework deployed felt a positive impact on EVA.

Impact of Organizational Competency Dictionary

The analysis of the cross tabulated data reveals that there is an impact of the use of a competency dictionary and EVA. Over 70% of the respondents in organizations with deployed competency management frameworks believe that the use of organizational competency dictionaries positively impacts EVA.

Competency dictionaries include all or most of the general competencies needed to cover all job families and competencies that are core or common to all jobs within an organization. These include competencies that are more closely related to the knowledge, skills and attributes (KSA) needed for specific jobs or functions. The demonstration of these competencies by employees and managers is related to increased performance at the individual, team, and organizational levels.

Research Implication - 4

This proves that the use of a Competency Dictionary positively impacts Employee Productivity and enhances Organizational Agility.

Impact of Organizational Competency Models

The cross tabulation of the use of Competency Models and Impact on Organizational EVA reveals that over 57% of the respondents in organizations with a competency management framework deployed opinion a positive impact of the use of competency models on organizational EVA. Most competency models include knowledge areas, skills, abilities, and other personal attributes (referred to as "KSAOs"). The structure of competency models can vary, but they usually have competency titles and specific behavioral descriptors which define the competencies. Some competency models define the competencies in terms of levels, such as core, intermediate, and advanced. A competency model helps to match the current workforce profile with the organization's performance requirements and onboard candidates with the right skills and proficiency levels to meet the current and future organizational requirements. A well designed competency model provides a basis for identifying and retaining critical skills and forms the foundation for increasing organizational intellectual capital. Further, use of competency models helps an organization save on recruitment costs, turnover costs (by developing a meaningful career plans), and training costs (by developing learning maps that tie competencies to training). This leads to enhanced employee engagement and hence reduces employee turnover.

Business performance is positively influenced by the commitment of its organizational members and their ability to generate new knowledge. This favorable performance level subsequently acts as a deterrent to turnover which in turn positively effects human capital management.

Research Implication - 5

It is thus evident that Competency Models leads to reduced Employee Turnover while positively impacting Business Performance

Impact of Organizational Competency Mapping

The cross tabulation of the use of Organizational Competency Mapping and Impact on Organizational EVA reveals that in excess of 52% of the respondents in organizations with a competency management framework deployed opinion a positive impact of the use of competency models on organizational EVA. Only 4% of the respondents felt that there was no co-relation between the use of competency mapping techniques and enhancement in Organizational EVA, while the remaining respondents were neutral.

Competency mapping is a strategic HR framework for monitoring the performance and development of human assets in organizations. Competency based talent management can improve both productivity and performance by identifying key characteristics of top performers and how those traits differ from average employees. These characteristics in turn can filter in a set of core competency profile that consistently leads to successful workforce. The remaining residual can further be developed into core competencies in some other functional areas, as HR philosophy has firm faith that people have potential and can be further nurtured if given proper environment and opportunities. Competency based Human Resource Management (HRM) is being increasingly recognized as an effective way of talent management over the previously adopted job-description related approach. It involves a transition from the traditional way of managing human resources based on what people have (e.g. Skills and abilities) to what people can do (performance). Effectively mapped competencies translate the strategic vision and goal of the organization into behavioural actions that employees must display. Competency based talent management concentrates first on the person and subsequently on their results.

Research Implication – 6

This proves that Organizational Competency Mapping positively impacts Employee Productivity, enhances its Strategic Capability while fostering employee innovation and enhanced organizational response to changes in business and customer environments.

Research Implication – 7

Organizational Competency Mapping and Management results in enhanced employee productivity, reduced employee turnover, innovation at the employee, departmental and organizational level, improved strategic capability, response to changes in external environment (agility) and hence sustainable Business Performance. All these factors results in increased EVA. Thus it can be conclusively established that Organizational Competency Mapping & Management process positively impacts its economic profits leading to enhanced

EVA.

HO5 Organizational Competency Mapping & Management has not enhanced the ability of Indian Business Enterprises to rapidly and cost effectively adapt to changing business and economic landscape

The constructs, the dimensions and the variables employed for testing the hypothesis is presented in table 5.10.

Table 5.10 – Hypothesis - 5 Dimensions

S.N	Construct	Dimension	Q No.
1	Status of Competency Mapping & Management in Indian Organizations	Competency Management Framework Deployment	12
2	Impact of Competency Mapping & Management	Strategic Capability	28
3	Impact of Competency Mapping & Management	Employee Productivity	29
4	Impact of Competency Mapping & Management	Employee Turnover	30
5	Impact of Competency Mapping & Management	Agility	31
6	Impact of Competency Mapping & Management	Innovation	32

Testing

The results of Kruskal-Wallis test for hypothesis is presented in the table 5.11. H5 is the summation of the Likert Scale Items (Q28 – Q32). H5 represents the Agility of an organization. It can be observed that the value of $p < 0.05$. This rejects the null hypothesis and accepts the alternative hypothesis.

Table 5.11 – Hypothesis-5 Testing – Independent Samples – Kruskal Wallis Test

Hypothesis Test Summary

	Null Hypothesis	Test	Sig.	Decision
1	The distribution of H5 is the same across categories of Q12.	Independent-Samples Kruskal-Wallis Test	.000	Reject the null hypothesis.

Asymptotic significances are displayed. The significance level is .05.

Organizational agility is a core differentiator in today's rapidly changing business environment. It is widely believed that organizations which are not agile are at a competitive disadvantage since it cannot anticipate and prepare for fundamental marketplace shifts (The Economist Intelligence Unit Limited, 2009).

Agility, on an organizational level, refers to efficiency with which an organization can respond to change. Agility incorporates the ideas of flexibility, balance, adaptability, and coordination under one umbrella. In a business context, agility typically refers to the ability of an organization to rapidly adapt to market and environmental changes in productive and cost-effective ways

Over 65% of the respondents believed that there is a positive linkage between the deployment of Competency Mapping and Management techniques and Organizational agility.

Research Implication - 8

Organizational Competency Mapping & Management enhances the ability of Indian Business Enterprises to rapidly and cost effectively adapt to changing business and economic landscape.

HO6 Indian Organizations have been not been able to increase employee engagement and provide superior value proposition (Employee Value Proposition – EVP) by virtue of deploying enterprise Competency Management

Framework

The constructs, the dimensions and the variables employed for testing the hypothesis is presented in table 5.12.

Table 5.12 – Hypothesis - 6 Dimensions

S.N	Construct	Dimension	Q No.
1	Status of Competency Mapping & Management in Indian Organizations	Competency Management Framework Deployment	12
2	Status of Competency Mapping & Management in Indian Organizations	Use of Competency Mapping Techniques	24
3	Impact of Competency Mapping & Management	Employee Productivity	29
4	Impact of Competency Mapping & Management	Employee Turnover	30
5	Impact of Competency Mapping & Management	Agility	31

Testing

The results of Wilcoxon Signed Ranks Test for hypothesis 6 are presented in the table 5.13. H6 is the summation of the Likert Scale Items (Q24, 29-31) and represents the Employee Value Proposition (EVP) of an organization. It can be observed that the value of $p < 0.05$. This rejects the null hypothesis and accepts the alternative hypothesis.

Table 5.13 – Hypothesis-6 Testing – Wilcoxon Signed Ranks Test

Test Statistics[a]		
	H6 - Q12	H6 - Q24
Z	-16.224[b]	-15.236[b]
Asymp. Sig. (2-tailed)	.000	.000
a. Wilcoxon Signed Ranks Test		
b. Based on negative ranks.		

The cross tabulation of the deployment of Organizational Competency Framework and its impact on EVP reveals that 69% of the respondents whose organizations have a competency framework deployed opinioned that there is a positive impact of Organizational Competency Management on EVP.

Employee Value Proposition (EVP) is the balance of the rewards and benefits that are received by employees in return for their performance at the workplace. (Michington, Your Employer Brand – attract, engage, retain, 2006) defines an Employee Value Proposition (EVP) as a set of associations and offerings provided by an organization in return for the skills, capabilities and experiences an employee brings to the organization. The EVP is an employee-centered approach that is aligned to existing, integrated workforce planning strategies because it has been informed by existing employees and the external target audience. An EVP must be unique, relevant and compelling if it is to act as a key driver of talent attraction, engagement and retention. (Michington, 2010). A superior EVP results in higher employee satisfaction, increase employee engagement and retention.

Research Implication - 9

It can thus be established that Indian Organizations have been able to increase employee engagement and provide superior value proposition (Employee Value Proposition – EVP) by virtue of deploying enterprise Competency Management Framework

HO7 Organizational Competency Mapping & Management does not call for substantial investments in terms of time to attain process maturity before realizing significant ROI

The constructs, the dimensions and the variables employed for testing the hypothesis is presented in table 5.14.

Table 5.14 – Hypothesis - 7 Dimensions

S.N	Construct	Dimension	Q No.
1	Status of Competency Mapping & Management in Indian Organizations	Competency Management Framework Deployment	12
2	Analysis of Competency Mapping & Management in Indian Organizations	Timeline for Organizational Competency Mapping & Management Deployment	33
3	Analysis of Competency Mapping & Management in Indian Organizations	Timeline for realizing Organizational Competency Mapping & Management ROI	34

Testing

The hypothesis testing results are presented in the table 5.15.. It can be observed that the value of $p < 0.05$. This rejects the null hypothesis and accepts the alternative hypothesis.

Table 5.15 – Hypothesis - 7 Testing – Kruskal Wallis Test

Test Statistics[a,b]		
	Q33	Q34
Chi-Square	19.666	28.210
df	1	1
Asymp. Sig.	.000	.000
a. Kruskal Wallis Test		
b. Grouping Variable: Q12		

One of the primary factors for measuring the effectiveness of

Organizational Human Capital Effectiveness is ROI. It is a performance measure used to evaluate the efficiency of an investment or to compare the efficiency of a number of different investments. In essence, organizations constantly strive to generate more revenue and income per employee. A low Employee Turnover will yield a higher base of organizational knowledge and less deterioration of experiential learning.

The cross tabulation of the time taken for deploying Organizational Competency Mapping & Management initiatives (Q33) and the minimum time period for realization of ROI (Q34) indicates that over 59% of the respondent's organizations have a Competency Management Framework and further over 70% of the respondents organizations have deployed Competency models. Over 30% of the respondents, whose organizations have a competency management framework, reported that it, took 6 months to a year for implementation and 57% of these respondents reported an ROI time line of a further 6 months to 1 year. 25% of the respondents reported an implementation time of 1 – 3 years with a timeline of 1- 3 years for realization of ROI.

Research Implication - 10

It can thus be inferred that Organizational Competency Mapping & Management requires substantial investments in terms of time to attain process maturity before realizing significant ROI.

HO8 *Organizational Competency Mapping & Management rarely leads to employee competency development and organizational capability enhancement and has no impact on Business Performance and does not enhance customer value or provide financial leverage*

The constructs, the dimensions and the variables employed for testing the hypothesis is presented in table 5.16.

Table 5.16 – Hypothesis - 8 Dimensions

S.N	Construct	Dimension	Q No.
1	Status of Competency Mapping & Management in Indian Organizations	Competency Management Framework Deployment	12
2	Impact of Competency Mapping & Management	Business Performance	27
3	Impact of Competency Mapping & Management	Strategic Capability	28
4	Impact of Competency Mapping & Management	Agility	31
5	Impact of Competency Mapping & Management	Innovation	32

Testing

The results of Mann-Whitney U test for hypothesis is presented in the table 5.17. H8 is the summation of the Likert Scale Items (Q27, Q28, Q31 & Q32). H8 the Customer Value Proposition of an organization. It can be observed that the value of p <0.05. This rejects the null hypothesis and accepts the alternative hypothesis.

Table 5.17 – Hypothesis -8 Testing – Mann-Whitney Test

Test Statistics[a]	
	H8
Mann-Whitney U	20272.000
Wilcoxon W	44582.000
Z	-11.050
Asymp. Sig. (2-tailed)	.000
a. Grouping Variable: Q12	

The cross tabulation of the use of Competency Management Frameworks (Q12) and Customer Value Proposition (CVP) indicates that 65% of the respondents whose organizations employ a Competency Mapping and Management framework believe that there is a strong positive impact on Customer Value Proposition.

A customer value proposition is a key differentiator of an organization that provides superior products or services. It is an indicator of the intrinsic value that the product or service delivered by a business enterprise. A product with a successful consumer value proposition is directly linked to a products actual and sustained performance versus competition (Investopedia, 2010). The two main attributes that allow consumers to differentiate among products are price and quality. Finding the correct balance between these two attributes usually leads to a successful product. If a company is able to produce the same quality product as its direct competition but sell it for less, this provides a price value to the consumer. Similarly, if a company is able to produce a superior quality product for the same or a slightly higher but acceptable price, the value to the consumer is added through the quality of the product. A product must offer value through price and/or quality in order to be successful (Lake, 2010). An enhanced Customer Value Proposition leads to a high positive branding for the organization. A brand is the perception of a product or service that is designed to stay in the minds of targeted consumers. This will help the organization to garner a high market share while ensuring sustained Business Performance.

Research Implication – 11

Organizational Competency Mapping & Management leads to employee competency development and organizational capability enhancement and has positive impact on Business Performance while enhancing customer value and providing high financial leverage

Conclusions

1. Competency Mapping & Management techniques are widely employed in Indian Business Enterprises
2. Competency Models are used for selection, training, performance appraisal and career planning by Indian Business Enterprises with deployed Competency Management Frameworks
3. Organizational Competency Mapping & Management has a

positive impact on its Strategic Capability
4. Organizational Competency Mapping & Management has a positive impact on Employee Productivity and Turnover
5. Organizational Competency Mapping & Management has a positive impact on Agility
6. Organizational Competency Mapping & Management has a positive impact on Innovation
7. Organizational Competency Mapping & Management has enhanced the ability of Indian Business Enterprises to rapidly and cost effectively adapt to changing business and economic landscape
8. Indian Organizations have been able to increase employee engagement and provide superior value proposition (Employee Value Proposition – EVP) by virtue of deploying enterprise Competency Management Frameworks
9. Organizational Competency Mapping & Management calls for substantial investments in terms of time to attain process maturity before realizing significant ROI
10. Organizational Competency Mapping & Management leads to employee competency development and organizational capability enhancement resulting in enhanced Business Performance, superior Customer Value Proposition (CVP) and high financial leverage
11. Best Practice Benchmarking of organizational competency mapping and management processes along with the use of standard competency models positively impact Business Performance
12. Organizational Competency Mapping & Management process strongly impact enterprise economic profits leading to enhanced EVA

6 COMPETENCE MANAGEMENT FRAMEWORK

6.0 Designing a Framework

The research framework contains the descriptions of research outputs and research activities (March & Smith, 1995). We can identify four research outputs and four research activities. The four research activities are: build, evaluate, theorize, and justify. The first two are activities of constructive research (design science), and the latter two are activities of descriptive research (natural science).

Building is the process of constructing an artefact for a specific purpose. In the building process, one develops constructs, models, methods and instantiations. Artefact performance is related to the environment in which it operates. A critical challenge in building an artefact is anticipating the potential side-effects of its use, and ensuring that unwanted side-effects are avoided.

Evaluation is the process of determining how well the artefact performs. "Evaluate refers to the development of criteria and the assessment of artefact performance against those criteria". The evaluate activity helps develop metrics and compares the performance of constructs, models, methods, and instantiations developed for specific tasks. Metrics are important in defining the research objectives. At a more detailed level, March & Smith identify the following evaluation metrics for the different artefacts:

- Evaluation of Constructs - Completeness, Simplicity, Elegance, Understandability, and Ease-of-Use
- Evaluation of Models - Fidelity with real world phenomena, Completeness, Level of Detail, robustness and internal consistency
- Evaluation of Methods - Operationality (ability to perform the intended task), Efficiency, Generality and Ease-of-Use
- Evaluation of Instantiations - Efficiency and Effectiveness of the artefact and its impacts on the environment and users

Theories explicate the characteristics of the artefact and its interaction with the environment that result in the observed performance. Theories explicate "why and how the constructs, models, methods, and instantiations work". "It may involve developing constructs with which to theorize about constructs, models, methods and instantiations". "Theorizing about models can be as simple as positing that a model used for designed purpose is true".

Justifying involves the testing of the developed theories by gathering evidence. The testing is generally performed based on mathematical and involves data collection and analysis. The entire concept is pictorially represented in figure 6.1.

This proposed framework is an outcome of the research work presented in this book and is mapped to the research framework presented in figure 6.1.

Build – The constructs were identified and built after extensive literature survey, discussions with experts in the field of knowledge and competency management and three pilot surveys. The key constructs for this research was presented in figure . The conceptual framework in the form of a set of working hypothesis is presented in figure 7.2. The theoretical and mathematical model based on the above constructs is presented in figure 7.3 and equation 1 respectively. The competency mapping and management methods are outlined in chapter 2 and the instantiations are provided in chapter 5 & 6.

Evaluate – The constructs were examined for reliability and validity. They exhibit strong internal reliability, Content validity, Factorial Validity – Convergent and Discriminant Validity and Construct Validity.

Theorize – The working of the constructs, its interaction with the environment and its observed performance is extensively covered in chapters 2, 5 and 6. The model is presented in detail in this chapter.

Justify – The testing of the constructs was done statistically as outlines in chapter 5.

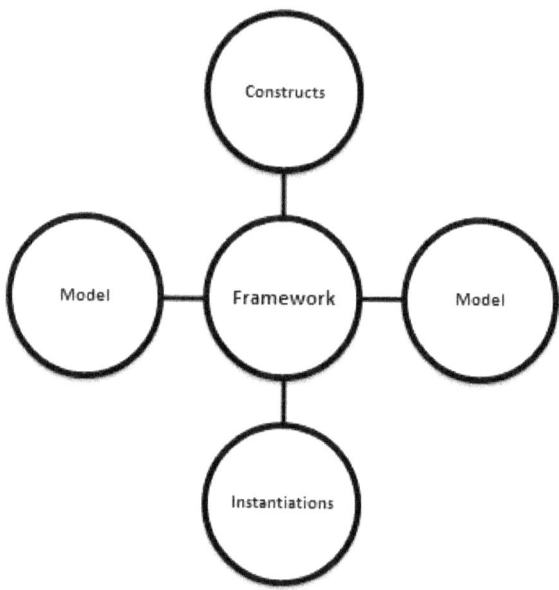

Figure 6.1 –Research Framework

Table 6.1 Research Constructs

S.N	Construct	Variables	No. of Questions	Questions
1	Demographic Profiling	8	8	Q3, Q5, Q6, Q7, Q8, Q9, Q10, Q11
2	Status of Competency Mapping & Management in Indian Organizations	4	4	Q12, Q13, Q14, Q24
3	Competency Mapping & Management Bench Marking Efforts in Indian Organizations	3	3	Q20, Q22, Q23
4	Analysis of Competency Mapping & Management in Indian Organizations	21	10	Q15, Q16, Q17, Q18, Q19, Q21, Q25, Q26, Q33, Q34
5	Impact of Competency Mapping & Management	7	7	Q27, Q28, Q29, Q30, Q31, Q32, Q35
6	Overall	43	32	

6.1 Conceptual Framework

Conceptual frameworks (theoretical frameworks) refer to the intermediate theory that attempt to connect to all aspects of inquiry (e.g., problem definition, purpose, literature review, methodology, data collection and analysis). Conceptual frameworks can act like maps that give coherence to empirical inquiry (Wikipedia). The working hypothesis is a type of conceptual framework. The conceptual framework for this research is presented in table 6.2. These are based on the deployment of various CMM initiatives and their organizational impact. The deployment of a holistic Organizational Competency Mapping & Management Framework positively impacts:

- Business Performance
- Strategic Capabilities
- Agility
- Employee Productivity
- Employee Turnover
- Innovation

Table 6.2 – Conceptual Research Framework

H_1	CMM Deployment
H_2	Competency Model Deployment
H_3	CMM Benchmarking
H_4	CMM & EVA
$H_{4.1}$	*CMM & Business Performance*
$H_{4.2}$	*CMM & Strategic Capability*
$H_{4.3}$	*Employee Productivity*
$H_{4.4}$	*Employee Turnover*
$H_{4.5}$	*Agility*
$H_{4.6}$	*CMM & Innovation*
H_5	CMM & Change Management
H_6	CMM & EVP
H_7	CMM & ROI
H_8	CMM & Organizational Capability, CVP

6.2 Statistical Modeling

A statistical model is a formalization of relationships between variables in the form of mathematical equations. A statistical model describes how one or more random variables are related to one or more other variables. The model is statistical as the variables are not deterministically but stochastically related. The model is a probability distribution constructed to enable inferences to be drawn or decisions made from data collected (Wikipedia, 2012).

The key feature of a statistical model is that variability is represented using probability distributions, which form the building-blocks from which the model is constructed. Typically it must accommodate both random and systematic variation. The randomness inherent in the probability distribution accounts for apparently haphazard scatter in the data, and systematic pattern is supposed to be generated by structure in the model. The art of modelling lies in finding a balance that enables the questions at hand to be answered or new ones posed. The complexity of the model will depend on the problem at hand and the answer required, so different models and analyses may be appropriate for a single set of data.

6.3 Research Model

The research model describes the overall framework presented in the above sections. The model presented in this study is a qualitative model designed from the constructs developed. The theoretical model is depicted in the figure 6.2.

An organizational framework is essential in order to integrate, synchronize and achieve positive synergy among individual, localized group competency initiatives. The figure 6.3 illustrates this concept. An organizational framework amplifies the tangible impact of the various competency initiatives resulting in superior EVA.

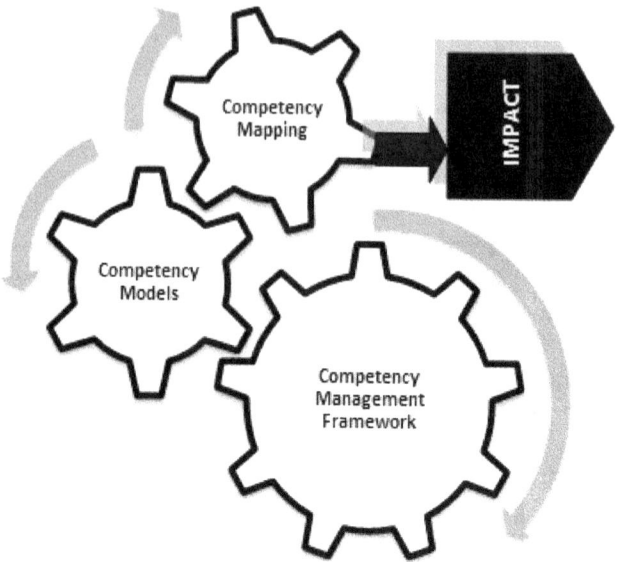

Figure 6.2 – Theoretical Competency Mapping and Management Model

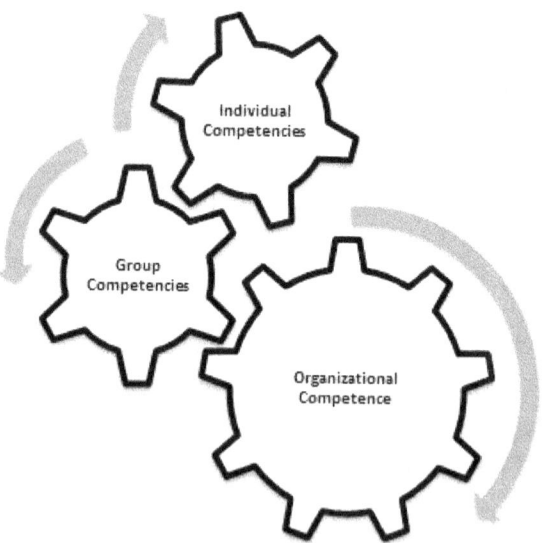

Figure 6.3 - Organizational Competence Development Cycle

The mathematical model for this research can be expressed by the equation 1:

$$y = a_o + \sum_{i=1}^{n} a_i v_i + b_i w_i + c_i x_i + d_i y_i + e_i z_i$$

Equation 1 – Mathematical CMM Model - Proposed

Where

y = *Impact of Organizational Competency & Management Initiatives*
v, w, x, y, z = *Independent variables*
a, b, c, d, e = *Competency Co-efficient*

y represents the Competency Deployment Index (CDI) which represents the tangible benefits accrued to an organization on the basis of its CMM initiatives.

It has been established in Chapter 5 and 6 that use of standardized competency models have a higher impact on organizational tangibles. Further benchmarking provides an organization with an effective reference to evaluate its own initiatives, undertake corrective action while providing an opportunity to study and incorporate global best practices.

Principal Component Analysis was performed on the key construct items and four factors were extracted. The four factors extracted represent the use of standardized models, competency mapping techniques, peer and global bench marking efforts and the use of organizational dictionaries and CMM framework. On the basis of the extracted values the actual mathematical model can be represented by Equation 2.

$$y = 6.975F1 + 1.676F2 + 1.234F3 + 1.034F4$$

Equation 2 – Mathematical CMM Model - Actual

Organizations that employ an holistic framework, use competency dictionaries, deploy standard models and continuously benchmark their efforts within their geographies as well as globally are among the most agile, innovative report the highest EVA. The concept is pictorially presented in figure 6.4.

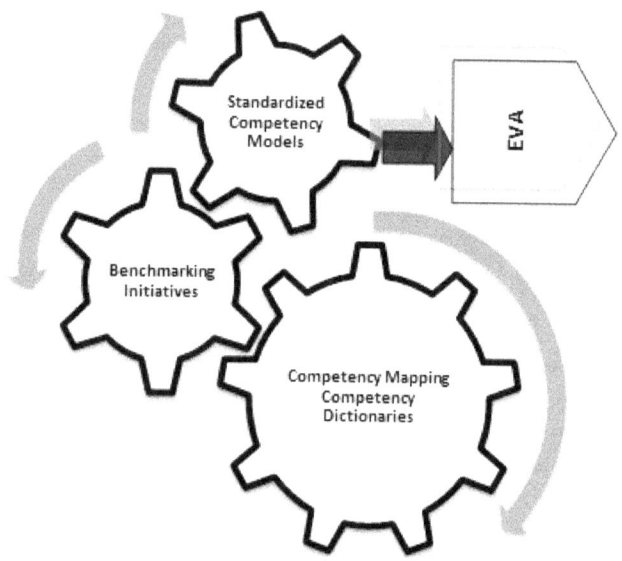

6.4 Organizational Competency Management – Key Constituents

6.4 Classification and Regression Tree Analysis

A partition analysis based on classification and regression tree (CART) was performed, prior to modeling, in order to understand the primary construct items impacting CDI. The analysis was performed using JMP Ver. 5.0 statistical analytical package from SAS.

Inferences

1. It is established that the use of standardized competency models has the maximum impact on CDI.
2. The next major contributor is the timeline for deploying organizational competency mapping and management initiatives.
3. The initiatives undertaken by an organization to benchmark its CMM initiatives also has a major impact on CDI. Peer benchmarking efforts have a greater impact on CDI.
4. Competency mapping is an integral part of organizational CMM activities. Organizations which employ competency mapping have a significantly higher EVA.
5. The type of competency models that are used also have a significant impact on the Business performance of an organization.
6. Competency mapping and management activities have a negligible impact when done in isolation – Group or Department wise. The benefits are significantly multiplied in organizations with a holistic Competency Management Framework.
7. While a organizational CMM framework is a prerequisite for realizing significant positive impact on all operational parameters, considerable ROI can be realized by initiating CM activities across multiple departments/divisions simultaneously.

6.5 Competence/Competency Models

Competencies are behaviors that encompass the knowledge, skills, and attributes required for successful performance at the workplace. In addition to intelligence and aptitude, the underlying characteristics of a person, such as traits, habits, motives, social roles, and self-image, as well as the environment around them, enable a person to deliver superior performance in a given job, role, or situation (Maggie LaRocca, 2011).

Competency modeling is the activity of determining the specific competencies that are characteristic of high performance and success in a given job. Competency modeling can be applied to a variety of human resource activities.

Conceptual Basis

A competency is a measurable human capability that is required for effective performance. A competency may be comprised of knowledge, a single skill or ability, a personal characteristic, or a cluster of two or more of these attributes. Competencies are the building blocks of work performance. The performance of most tasks requires the simultaneous or sequenced demonstration of multiple competencies (Hoge, Tondora, & Marrelli, 2005).

Knowledge is awareness, information, or understanding about facts, rules, principles, guidelines, concepts, theories, or processes needed to successfully perform a task (Marrelli, 2001; Mirabile, 1997). The knowledge may be concrete, specific, and easily measurable, or more complex, abstract, and difficult to assess (Lucia & Lepsinger, 1999). Knowledge is acquired through learning and experience.

A skill is a capacity to perform mental or physical tasks with a specified outcome (Marrelli, 1998). Similar to knowledge, skills can range from highly concrete and easily identifiable tasks, such as filing documents alphabetically, to those that are less tangible and more abstract, such as managing a quality improvement project (Hoge, Tondora, & Marrelli, in press; Lucia & Lepsinger, 1999). An ability is a demonstrated cognitive or physical capability to successfully perform a task with a wide range of possible outcomes (Marrelli, 1998).

Ability is a constellation of several underlying capacities that enable an individual to learn and perform. These are often time-consuming and difficult to develop, and usually have a strong component of innate capacity.

Developing Competency Models

The development of competency models is a critical factor in determining the future success of an organization. Competencies enable employees to achieve results, thereby creating value. It follows that competencies aligned with business objectives help foster an organization's success. Organizations must understand their core competency needs - the skills, knowledge, behaviors, and abilities that are necessary for people in key roles to deliver business results. The identification and application of the competencies required for effective job performance has become a complex and sophisticated endeavor as experience with this approach has furthered across business enterprises globally.

During the course of this research extensive work was undertaken to study, define, measure and evaluate the core organizational, group as well as individual competencies. This was supplemented with comprehensive Behavioral Elicitation Interviews (BEI), Competency Elicitation Interviews (CEI) and pilot testing. The figure 7.26 illustrates the model design and development methodology.

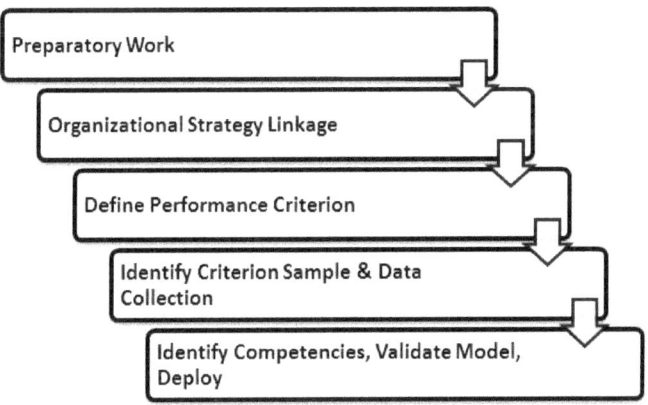

Figure 6.5 - Developing a Competency Model

Preparatory Work

This stage involves identifying jobs that are important from an organizations strategic perspective. This can be implemented through a study of the organization's Annual Operating Plan (AOP) and interviewing the leadership team

Organizational Strategy Linkage

This process involves reviewing the organization's Mission, isolating critical success factors and developing strategic plans for achieving the goals

Performance Criterion Definition

This step involves the identification of performance measures or criteria that define effective job performance.

Criterion Sample Identification

The measures developed in the above step can be used to validate the measures on a sample population from a division/department/group. The sample size should be a minimum of 20 and include 12 superior and 8 average performers. Statistical tests of hypotheses including t-tests, chi-square or ANOVA can be used for validation.

Data Collection

The following are some of the common methods used for data collection:
1. Behavioural Elicitation Interviews (BEI)
2. Expert Panels
3. Surveys
4. 360o Feedback
5. Observation
6. Competency Identification & Model Development

The data collected from all the above sources are analyzed to identify the personalities and skill competencies that distinguish superior from average performers. This process is referred to as hypothesis generation, thematic analysis or concept formation.

Model Validation

In order to validate the developed model, BEI data is collected on a second criterion sample of superior and average performers. This sample is scored and the results validated from the predictions of the first model. This approach is referred to as concurrent cross validation.

Model Deployment

Once the model has been validated it can be used as the basis for talent acquisition, assessment centers, performance management, succession planning, learning & development as well as organizational reward & recognition schemes.

On the basis of this exhaustive study a competency model was developed and deployed in a leading telecom organization in India. A snapshot of this model is presented in table 6.3.

Table 6.3 – Competency Model for Telcos

	Competency Model for Telcos			
Role	Generic & Behavioural Competencies	Managerial Competencies	Leadership Competencies	Functional Competencies
TECHNOLOGY HEAD	Talent Development, Customer Service Orientation, Interpersonal Understanding, Concern for Order, Communication, Judgment, Persistence, Mentoring, Resilience, Credibility, Integrity & Sincerity, Diversity, Self-Control, Self Discipline	Impact & Influence, Achievement Orientation, Teamwork & Co-operation, Analytical Thinking, Directiveness/Assertiveness, Information Seeking, Team Leadership, Conceptual Thinking, Organizational Awareness, Relationship Building, Specialized Knowledge, Cost Management, Budgeting, Financial Management	Initiative, Actionable Opportunities, Persistence, Information Management, Concern for High Quality Work, Commitment to Work Contract, Efficiency Orientation, Systematic Planning, Problem Solving, Self Confidence, Persuasion, Use of Influence Strategies, Assertiveness, Strategic Analysis, Strategic Planning, Strategic Thinking & Scenario Building, Building Intellectual Capital, Mediation & Negotiation	Technology & Service Architecture, Market Trends & Developments, Product & Services Evaluation & Integration Model - Awareness, TRAI & WPC Regulatory Compliance - Awareness, Wireless & Wireline Technologies (CDMA, GSM, 3G, SDH, DWDM, OTN, FWA, FA, NGN, Data Networks /MEN/HSD), Fiber Plant & Utility Management, Network Resource Optimization, Human Capital Management

OPERATIONS LEAD	Talent Development, Customer Service Orientation, Interpersonal Understanding, Self Confidence, Concern for Order, Communication, Judgment, Persistence, Mentoring, Resilience, Credibility, Integrity & Sincerity	Financial Management, Budgeting, Stress Management, Technology Management, Flexibility	Initiative, Actionable Opportunities, Persistence, Information Management, Concern for High Quality Work, Commitment to Work Contract, Efficiency Orientation, Self Confidence, Persuasion, Use of Influence Strategies, Assertiveness, Strategic Thinking & Scenario Building, Building Intellectual Capital, Mediation & Negotiation	Wireless & Wireline Telecom Network Architecture (Circuit & Packet), Traffic Analysis, Capacity Planning, ,BoM Verification, Service Architecture, Technology Updation, Network RCA, MS Contract Management
PLANNING & ENGG HEAD	Talent Development, Customer Service Orientation, Interpersonal Understanding, Self Confidence, Concern for Order, Communication, Judgment, Credibility, Integrity & Sincerity, Diversity, Self Discipline	Achievement Orientation, Teamwork & Co-operation, Analytical Thinking, Directiveness/Assertiveness, Information Seeking, Team Leadership, Conceptual Thinking, Organizational Awareness, Knowledge, Cost Management	Actionable Opportunities, Persistence, Information Management, Concern for High Quality Work, Commitment to Work Contract, Efficiency Orientation, Systematic Planning, Problem Solving, Self Confidence, Persuasion, Use of Influence Strategies, Assertiveness, Strategic Analysis, Strategic Planning,	Wireless & Wireline Telecom Network Architecture (Circuit & Packet), Capacity Planning (Wireless & Wireline), Network Optimization (Wireless & Wireline), Traffic Analysis, Inventory Management, Industry Trends & Best Practices, Vendor & New Product Evaluation

TECHNOLOGY & BUSINESS STRATEGY HEAD	Customer Service Orientation, Interpersonal Understanding, Self Confidence, Concern for Order, Communication, Judgment, Persistence,	Impact & Influence, Achievement Orientation, Teamwork & Co-operation, Analytical Thinking, Directiveness/Assertiveness, Information Seeking, Team Leadership, Conceptual Thinking, Organizational Awareness, Relationship Building, Specialized Knowledge, Cost Management, Financial Management, Budgeting, Stress Management, Technology Management, Flexibility	Initiative, Actionable Opportunities, Persistence, Information Management, Concern for High Quality Work, Efficiency Orientation, Systematic Planning, Self Confidence, Persuasion, Use of Influence Strategies, Assertiveness, Strategic Thinking & Scenario Building, Building Intellectual Capital,	Technology & Product Trends & Developments, Product & Services Evaluation & Integration, TRAI & WPC Regulatory Compliance, Security Models - 3GPP, 3GPP2, CISSP, CISA, ISO27001 LA.
COMMERCIAL & INMM HEAD	Talent Development, Customer Service Orientation, Interpersonal Understanding, Self Confidence, Concern for Order, Communication, Judgment, Persistence, Mentoring, Resilience, Credibility, Integrity & Sincerity	Financial Management, Budgeting, Stress Management, Flexibility, Cost Management, Organizational Awareness	Initiative, Actionable Opportunities, Persistence, Information Management, Concern for High Quality Work, Capital Mediation, Commitment to Work Contract, Efficiency Orientation, Negotiation, Persuasion, Use of Influence Strategies, Assertiveness, Strategic Thinking & Scenario Building, Building IC	Inventory Management - JIT, SAP-FICO & MM, SCM, Contract Management, Telecom Equipment/Product Overview

HR & LEARNING AND DEVELOPMENT HEAD	Talent Development, Customer Service Orientation, Interpersonal Understanding, Confidence, Concern for Order, Communication, Judgment, Persistence, Mentoring, Resilience, Credibility, Integrity & Sincerity	Impact & Influence, Achievement Orientation, Teamwork & Co-operation, Analytical Thinking, Directiveness/Assertiveness, Information Seeking, Team Leadership, Conceptual Thinking, Organizational Awareness, Relationship Building, Specialized Knowledge, Cost Management,	Initiative, Actionable Opportunities, Persistence, Information Management, Concern for High Quality Work, Commitment to Work Contract, Efficiency Orientation, Self Confidence, Persuasion, Use of Influence Strategies, Assertiveness, Strategic Thinking & Scenario Building, Building Intellectual Capital, Mediation & Negotiation	Talent Acquisition, Performance Management, Talent Management, Talent Development, Organizational Development, Human Capital Management, HR Tools - Hays Model, Psychometric Profiling, Competency Modelling, Telecom Network Architecture - Wireline & Wireless
EXECUTIVE ASSISTANT	Customer Service Orientation, Interpersonal Understanding, Confidence, Communication, Persistence, Resilience, Credibility, Integrity & Sincerity	Achievement Orientation, Teamwork & Co-operation, Analytical Thinking, Directiveness/Assertiveness, Information Seeking, Conceptual Thinking, Organizational Awareness, Relationship Building,	Initiative, Persistence, Information Management, Concern for High Quality Work, Efficiency Orientation, Self Confidence, Persuasion, Use of Influence Strategies, Assertiveness, Mediation & Negotiation	Telecom Network Architecture - Awareness, Productivity & Reporting Tools- MS Office Suite, SAP - Awareness

SECRETARY	Customer Service Orientation, Interpersonal Understanding, Confidence, Communication, Persistence, Resilience, Credibility, Integrity & Sincerity	Teamwork & Co-operation, Information Seeking, Organizational Awareness, Relationship Building,	-	In-Depth Knowledge of MS Office Suite, SAP - Awareness
OPERATIONS LEAD	Talent Development, Customer Service Orientation, Interpersonal Understanding, Self Confidence, Concern for Order, Communication, Judgment, Persistence	Teamwork & Co-operation, Analytical Thinking, Directiveness/Assertiveness, Information Seeking, Team Leadership, Conceptual Thinking,	Persistence, Information Management, Concern for High Quality Work, Commitment to Work Contract, Efficiency Orientation, Systematic Planning, Problem Solving, Self Confidence,	KPI Tracking & Improvement - Circuit & Packet Switched Network, Product Integration & Issues Resolution, IUC/RA Resolution
PLANNING LEAD	Talent Development, Customer Service Orientation, Interpersonal Understanding, Self Confidence, Concern for Order, Communication, Judgment, Persistence	Teamwork & Co-operation, Analytical Thinking, Directiveness/Assertiveness, Information Seeking, Team Leadership, Conceptual Thinking,	Concern for High Quality Work, Commitment to Work Contract, Efficiency Orientation, Systematic Planning, Problem Solving, Self Confidence, Persuasion, Strategic Analysis, Strategic Planning,	Call Routing & Switching System Architecture, Wireless Technologies & Standards, CDMA, GPRS, UMTS, LTE System Operations, IP Network Architecture, System Design, Review & Optimization, Voice Call Routing, s Technology Evaluation, Product & Vendor Evaluation

OPS PLANNING ENGINEER	Customer Service Orientation, Interpersonal Understanding, Confidence, Communication, Persistence, Resilience, Credibility, Integrity & Sincerity	Teamwork & Co-operation, Information Seeking, Organizational Awareness, Relationship Building,	-	Call Routing & Switching System - Awareness, Wireless Technologies & Standards, CDMA, GPRS, UMTS, LTE System Operations, IP Network Architecture, System Design, Review & Optimization, Voice Call Routing, s Technology Evaluation, Product & Vendor Evaluation
PROJECT LEAD	Talent Development, Customer Service Orientation, Interpersonal Understanding, Self Confidence, Concern for Order, Communication, Judgment, Persistence	Teamwork & Co-operation, Analytical Thinking, Directiveness/Assertiveness, Information Seeking, Conceptual Thinking, Organizational Awareness, Cost Management, Financial Management, Budgeting,	Persistence, Information Management, Concern for High Quality Work, Commitment to Work Contract, Efficiency Orientation, Systematic Planning, Problem Solving, Self Confidence,	Telecom Network Architecture, Design Tools - AutoCAD, SAP - Awareness, Site Design - Electrical, Mechanical, Civil
PROJECTS ENGINEER	Customer Service Orientation, Interpersonal Understanding, Confidence, Communication, Persistence, Resilience, Credibility, Integrity & Sincerity	Teamwork & Co-operation, Information Seeking, Organizational Awareness, Relationship Building,	-	Telecom Network Architecture, Design Tools - AutoCAD, SAP - Awareness, Site Design - Electrical, Mechanical, Civil

COMPETENCY MAPPING & MANAGEMENT – *A Comprehensive Survey*

O&M LEAD	Talent Development, Customer Service Orientation, Interpersonal Understanding, Self Confidence, Concern for Order, Communication, Judgment, Persistence	Teamwork & Co-operation, Analytical Thinking, Directiveness/Assertiveness, Information Seeking, Conceptual Thinking, Organizational Awareness, Cost Management, Financial Management, Budgeting,	Information Management, Concern for High Quality Work, Commitment to Work Contract, Efficiency Orientation, Systematic Planning, Problem Solving,	Optical Transport, Microwave & VSAT OAM, OFC OAM, OPEX Planning & Management, Vendor AMC Management, GSM, CDMA, Data Network Architecture, HSE&F Practices Implementation
NETWORK OPERATIONS - MANAGER (VENDOR)	Talent Development, Customer Service Orientation, Interpersonal Understanding, Self Confidence, Concern for Order, Communication, Judgment, Persistence	Teamwork & Co-operation, Analytical Thinking, Directiveness/Assertiveness, Information Seeking, Conceptual Thinking, Organizational Awareness, Cost Management, Financial Management, Budgeting,	Initiative, Persistence, Information Management, Commitment to Work Contract, Efficiency Orientation, Problem Solving, Persuasion, Use of Influence Strategies, Assertiveness,	In-depth Understanding of SDH ,DWDM, Microwave ,LMDS ,UBR ,DLC ,MEN ,DCN & Data Networks, L3VPN, MPLS, Routing Protocols - BGP, OSPF,RIP, EIGRP, Switching, EMS & NMS Management, Audit of High/Low Cap Transmission Networks, SLA & End-to-End Network Monitoring
TRANSMISSION LEAD	Talent Development, Customer Service Orientation, Interpersonal Understanding, Self Confidence, Concern for Order, Communication, Judgment, Persistence	Teamwork & Co-operation, Analytical Thinking, Directiveness/Assertiveness, Information Seeking, Team Leadership, Conceptual Thinking, Organizational Awareness,	Initiative, Persistence, Information Management, Commitment to Work Contract, Efficiency Orientation, Problem Solving, Persuasion, Use of Influence Strategies,	SLA & MTTR Management, OFC Network OAM, In-depth Knowledge of OFC, OTDR Operations, Splicing Techniques, Joint Closures, LSPM, SMPS, DG Sets, AC,

		Specialized Knowledge, Technology Management, Flexibility	Assertiveness,	Telecom Network Architecture
TRANSMISSION MANAGER	Talent Development, Customer Service Orientation, Interpersonal Understanding, Self Confidence, Communication, Judgment, Persistence	Teamwork & Co-operation, Conceptual Thinking, Directiveness/Assertiveness, Information Management, Team Leadership, Conceptual Thinking, Flexibility	Initiative, Persistence, Information Management, Commitment to Work Contract, Efficiency Orientation, Problem Solving, Persuasion,	SLA & MTTR Management, OFC Network OAM, In-depth Knowledge of OFC, OTDR Operations, Splicing Techniques, Joint Closures, LSPM, SMPS, DG Sets, AC, Telecom Network Architecture
NLD ENGG.	Customer Service Orientation, Interpersonal Understanding, Confidence, Communication, Persistence, Resilience, Credibility, Integrity & Sincerity	Teamwork & Co-operation, Information Seeking, Organizational Awareness, Relationship Building,	-	OFC Network OAM Process & Procedures, In-depth Knowledge of OFC, OTDR Operations, Splicing Techniques, Joint Closures, LSPM, SMPS, DG Sets, AC, Telecom Network Architecture

COMPETENCY MAPPING & MANAGEMENT – A Comprehensive Survey

Role				
FIXED ACCESS NETWORK LEAD	Talent Development, Customer Service Orientation, Interpersonal Understanding, Self Confidence, Concern for Order, Communication, Judgment, Persistence	Teamwork & Co-operation, Analytical Thinking, Directiveness/Assertiveness, Information Seeking, Team Leadership, Conceptual Thinking, Organizational Awareness, Specialized Knowledge, Technology Management, Flexibility	Initiative, Actionable Opportunities, Persistence, Information Management, Concern for High Quality Work, Commitment to Work Contract, Efficiency Orientation, Systematic Planning, Problem Solving, Self Confidence, Persuasion, Use of Influence Strategies, Assertiveness, Strategic Analysis, Strategic Planning, Strategic Thinking & Scenario Building, Building Intellectual Capital, Mediation & Negotiation	Knowledge of IP V4/6, MEN, LMDS, UBR, Wi-Max Networks, Knowledge of SDH, DWDM, Microwave Networks, OSS/BSS, SAP
FIXED ACCESS NETWORK MANAGER	Talent Development, Customer Service Orientation, Interpersonal Understanding, Self Confidence, Communication, Judgment, Persistence	Teamwork & Co-operation, Conceptual Thinking, Directiveness/Assertiveness, Information Management, Team Leadership, Conceptual Thinking, Flexibility	Initiative, Persistence, Information Management, Commitment to Work Contract, Efficiency Orientation, Problem Solving, Persuasion,	In-Depth Knowledge of IP V4/6, MEN, LMDS, UBR, Wi-Max Networks, Knowledge of SDH, DWDM, Microwave Networks, OSS/BSS, SAP

FIXED ACCESS NETWORK ENGINEER	Customer Service Orientation, Interpersonal Understanding, Confidence, Communication, Persistence, Resilience, Credibility, Integrity & Sincerity	Teamwork & Co-operation, Information Seeking, Organizational Awareness, Relationship Building,	-	IP V4/6, MEN, LMDS, UBR, Wi-Max Networks, Knowledge of SDH, DWDM, Microwave Networks, OSS/BSS, SAP
QUALITY & PERFORMANCE LEAD	Talent Development, Customer Service Orientation, Interpersonal Understanding, Self Confidence, Concern for Order, Communication, Judgment, Persistence	Teamwork & Co-operation, Analytical Thinking, Directiveness/Assertiveness, Information Seeking, Team Leadership, Conceptual Thinking, Organizational Awareness, Specialized Knowledge, Technology Management, Flexibility	Information Management, Concern for High Quality Work, Commitment to Work Contract, Efficiency Orientation, Strategic Analysis,	Network Quality & Performance Analysis, TRAI/TERM Regulatory Compliances, Network Architecture, Operations & Optimization - Wireless & Wireline Network, Drive Tests Analysis, Quality Models, Frameworks & Quality Standards
QUALITY & PERFORMANCE MANAGER	Talent Development, Customer Service Orientation, Interpersonal Understanding, Self Confidence, Communication, Judgment, Persistence	Teamwork & Co-operation, Analytical Thinking, Conceptual Thinking, Directiveness/Assertiveness, Information Management, Team Leadership, Conceptual Thinking, Flexibility	Initiative, Persistence, Information Management, Commitment to Work Contract, Efficiency Orientation, Problem Solving, Persuasion,	Quality Policy Formulation, Regulatory compliances/TRAI/TERM Cell Audits, IR/FAR Recommendations Implementation

QUALITY & PERFORMANCE ENGINEER	Customer Service Orientation, Interpersonal Understanding, Confidence, Communication, Persistence, Resilience, Credibility, Integrity & Sincerity	Teamwork & Co-operation, Information Seeking, Organizational Awareness, Relationship Building,	-	Analysis Tools, Quality & Performance Analysis, Regulatory Compliances - TRAI, Rogue cells Tracking & Optimisation, Drive Test Based Optimisation Implementation
WIRELESS PLANNING LEAD	Talent Development, Customer Service Orientation, Interpersonal Understanding, Self Confidence, Concern for Order, Communication, Judgment, Persistence	Teamwork & Co-operation, Analytical Thinking, Directiveness/Assertiveness, Information Seeking, Team Leadership, Conceptual Thinking, Organizational Awareness, Specialized Knowledge, Technology Management, Flexibility	Initiative, Persistence, Information Management, Concern for High Quality Work Systematic Planning, Problem Solving, Self Confidence, Strategic Analysis, Strategic Planning, Strategic Thinking & Scenario Building	Telecommunication Fundamentals - GSM, CDMA, 3G, Network architecture & Parameters- GSM, CDMA, 3G, Planning & Optimization tools for ACP & AFP - TCPU, ATOLL, Optmi, Schema, NASTAR, Drive Test, Drive Test Log Analysis & Post processing, CW Testing, MapInfo

WIRELESS PLANNING MANAGER	Talent Development, Customer Service Orientation, Interpersonal Understanding, Self Confidence, Communication, Judgment, Persistence	Teamwork & Co-operation, Conceptual Thinking, Directiveness/Assertiveness, Information Management, Team Leadership, Conceptual Thinking, Flexibility	Initiative, Persistence, Information Management, Commitment to Work Contract, Efficiency Orientation, Problem Solving, Persuasion,	RCA, ACP/AFP Planning & Optimization tools - TCPU, ATOLL, Optmi, Schema, NASTAR, CW Testing, Map Info, MS Office - Access, Visio, Project, Excel
WIRELESS PLANNING ENGINEER	Customer Service Orientation, Interpersonal Understanding, Confidence, Communication, Persistence, Resilience, Credibility, Integrity & Sincerity	Teamwork & Co-operation, Information Seeking, Organizational Awareness, Relationship Building,	-	Layer -3 Analysis, Network Diagnostics - Actix Post Processing Software, Spectrum Management, Frequency Planning, Interference Management, ACP/AFP Planning & Optimization tools - TCPU, ATOLL, Optmi, Schema, NASTAR, CW Testing, Map Info, MS Office - Access, Visio, Project, Excel

MICRO WAVE PLANN ING LEAD	Talent Development, Customer Service Orientation, Interpersonal Understanding, Self Confidence, Concern for Order, Communication, Judgment, Persistence	Teamwork & Co-operation, Analytical Thinking, Directiveness/Assertiveness, Information Seeking, Team Leadership, Conceptual Thinking, Organizational Awareness, Specialized Knowledge, Technology Management, Flexibility	Initiative, Persistence, Information Management, Concern for High Quality Work Systematic Planning, Problem Solving, Self Confidence, Strategic Analysis, Strategic Planning, Strategic Thinking & Scenario Building	End-to-End MW Transmission Planning - Access and Back Bone Network (Urban > 1000 Hops), MW link budget Designing, Interference Analysis using PDH & SDH radios - 6/7/15/18 GHz band, Network Optimization, Frequency Planning & Frequency Optimization, In-depth Skills on Pathloss4.0, Mapinfo, MS Excel & MW Radio Architecture, LOS Surveys, Survey Of India Topo Maps for BB design, IP Planning, NMS Integration Planning

MICROWAVE PLANNING MANAGER	Talent Development, Customer Service Orientation, Interpersonal Understanding, Self Confidence, Communication, Judgment, Persistence	Teamwork & Co-operation, Conceptual Thinking, Directiveness/Assertiveness, Information Management, Team Leadership, Conceptual Thinking, Flexibility	Initiative, Persistence, Information Management, Commitment to Work Contract, Efficiency Orientation, Problem Solving, Persuasion,	MW link budget Designing, Interference Analysis - PDH & SDH radios - 6/7/15/18/23 GHz band, Network Optimization, Frequency Planning & Frequency Optimization, In-depth Skills on Pathloss4.0, Mapinfo, MS Excel & MW Radio Architecture, LOS Surveys, Survey Of India Topo Maps for BB design, IP Planning, Microwave Regulatory Compliance - WPC/SACFA, Link Budget Design, NMS Integration
MICROWAVE PLANNING ENGINEER	Customer Service Orientation, Interpersonal Understanding, Confidence, Communication, Persistence, Resilience, Credibility, Integrity & Sincerity	Teamwork & Co-operation, Information Seeking, Organizational Awareness, Relationship Building,	-	Interference Analysis - PDH & SDH radios - 6/7/15/18/23 GHz band, Network Optimization, Frequency Planning & Frequency Optimization, In-depth Skills on Pathloss4.0, MapInfo, MS Excel & MW Radio Architecture, LOS Surveys, Survey Of India Topo

					Maps for BB design, Vendor Management, NMS Integration
CORE PLANNING LEAD	Talent Development, Customer Service Orientation, Interpersonal Understanding, Self Confidence, Concern for Order, Communication, Judgment, Persistence	Teamwork & Co-operation, Analytical Thinking, Directiveness/Assertiveness, Information Seeking, Team Leadership, Conceptual Thinking, Organizational Awareness, Specialized Knowledge, Technology Management, Flexibility	Initiative, Persistence, Information Management, Concern for High Quality Work Systematic Planning, Problem Solving, Self Confidence, Strategic Analysis, Strategic Planning, Strategic Thinking & Scenario Building		CA, PS & NGN Core Architecture, Vendor Evaluation & Management, RFP/SOW, Network Performance, Congestion & KPI Management, Business Solutions Development, Wireline Switch Engineering & Optimization, Product Development - Wireless & Wireline IN, VAS & SDP, Network Security Monitoring & Management, Platform certification & ATP Clearances

CORE PLANNING MANAGER	Talent Development, Customer Service Orientation, Interpersonal Understanding, Self Confidence, Communication, Judgment, Persistence	Teamwork & Co-operation, Conceptual Thinking, Directiveness/Assertiveness, Information Management, Team Leadership, Conceptual Thinking, Flexibility	Initiative, Persistence, Information Management, Commitment to Work Contract, Efficiency Orientation, Problem Solving, Persuasion,	Network Topology & Architecture Evaluation, Wireline & NGN Network - Operations Support, Operation Support & Performance Assurance - Packet Core Switches, HLR, STP, AAA, BG, Fire Wall, DNS, LNS, 2CNO Implementation, Platform Rollout, IT/BSS Integration, Certification & ATP
CORE PLANNING ENGINEER	Customer Service Orientation, Interpersonal Understanding, Confidence, Communication, Persistence, Resilience, Credibility, Integrity & Sincerity	Teamwork & Co-operation, Information Seeking, Organizational Awareness, Relationship Building,	-	Optimization of Platform capacities, ICD Closure, Service KPI Monitoring, Product UAT /Certification, AOP & Project Expansions BoM, Technical CARs, Budget & PR approval, Network Inventory & integrity checks

Inferences

The organizational Competency Management Initiatives have the most positive impact on CDI. The most commonly deployed organizational competency management initiatives are:
1. Competency Based Recruitment – 69.2%
2. Competency Based Role Mapping – 38.5%

3. Competency Based Employee Performance Management – 33.3%
4. Competency Based Internal Job Transfers – 25.6%

Benchmarking initiatives have a positive impact on organizational EVA. This concept has been covered in Chapter 6. Peer benchmarking initiatives (Predictor importance – 2) has been ranked higher those Global benchmarking initiatives (Predictor importance – 7)

The use of an organizational competency dictionary impacts CDI (Predictor importance – 3). It ensures the positive alignment and synergy among individual, group and organizational competencies.

The use of standardized models (Predictor Importance – 6) enhances the effectiveness of the competency mapping and management initiatives. Over 70% of the organizations surveyed employed competency models. Of these 30% of the organizations employed standard models. The models that have significant impact on CDI include:

1. Organizational Approach Model – 46.2%
2. Individualistic Approach Model – 15.4%
3. HR System Approach Model – 12.8%

It can be seen that the Organizational Approach Model is the most widely used competency model used by organizations.

The use of competency mapping techniques positively impact CDI. 69% of the organizations employ competency mapping techniques. The most popular techniques include:

1. Work Profile System (WPS) – 38.2%
2. Position Information Questionnaire (PIQ) – 25.5%
3. Competency Elicitation Interview (CEI) – 12.8%
4. Behavioural Elicitation Interview (BEI) – 7.7%
5. Occupational Analysis Inventory (OAI) – 7.7%
6. Multi-purpose Occupational Analysis Interview (MOSAIC) – 2.6%
7. Critical Incident Technique (CIT) – 0.2%
8. Common Metric Questionnaire (CMQ) – 0.2%
9. PIQ + OAI +WPS – 21.6%
10. PIQ + WBS – 22.9%
11. OAI + WPS – 10%

The use of standard competency models is a prerequisite to

realizing the benefits of competency mapping and management initiatives. This is supplemented by employing competency mapping techniques. Extensive peer benchmarking is essential during the early stages of CM implementation. Once the initiatives are firmly entrenched the organization should benchmark its activities with global enterprises. This facilitates transfer of industry specific global best practices. The design and deployment of a competency dictionary is mandatory to ensure synergy of individual, group and organizational competencies. All the CMM activities will not be fruitful in isolation and needs to be cemented through a holistic organizational framework.

7 CONTRIBUTIONS TO THEORY, PRACTICE, POLICY & TECHNOLOGY

7.0 Research Interpretations

This research presents a comprehensive status on the Competency Mapping and Management (CMM) activities in Indian Business Enterprises. It has been able to empirically validate the significant benefits of CMM initiatives. The following is the gist of the key results of this research:

1. The linkage between CMM and Organizational EVA, HVA, Agility, Strategic Capability and Innovation in the Indian industry has been conclusively established through this research work.
2. This research has also contributed to the development Organizational Competency Mapping and Management frameworks, competency models and has identified the key factors that maximize the impact of CMM initiatives within an organization.
3. The first evidence of linkages between the use of competency frameworks, standardized models, competency mapping techniques, benchmarking initiatives and their impact on EVA, in the Indian Industry has been established.

4. In many organizations, especially in India, CMM initiatives have been launched with much fanfare, but have been subsequently put on a backburner. This study has highlighted that minimum time required to implement organizational CMM initiatives (that bring about some tangible change) is 6 months. Further an additional minimum period of 6 months is required to realize tangible ROI.
5. Additionally in large organizations (with more than 10,000 employees) it would take a minimum period of three years to establish the entire CMM value chain and realizing significant ROI.
6. The work has brought out a set of recommendations for implementing and evaluating Organizational CMM and gathered evidence of their applicability.
7. Lastly this research work has systematically uncovered the key factors that define the success of CMM. It has also helped in designing and validating a functional competency model for the telecom industry.

7.1 Primary Findings

A. Competency Mapping & Management in Indian Organizations

1. 59% of the respondents surveyed reported the deployment of Competency Management Frameworks within their organizations
2. 33% respondents reported that there was no CM framework in their organizations
3. It is however to important to note that out of this 33% over 23% had some form of CM initiatives in their respective organizations.
4. 8 % of the respondents were not clear on the CM deployment status within their organizations

B. Competency Mapping & Management Bench Marking Efforts in Indian Organizations

1. 72% of the survey respondents reported the use of

competency models in their respective work place.
2. Only 18% of the respondents have reported peer benchmarking of competency mapping and management initiatives (CMM) efforts in their respective organizations.
3. Only 4% of the senior and top management have reported peer benchmarking of CMM initiatives in their organizations.
4. Thus it can be inferred that most of the Indian organizations do not benchmark their CMM activities with their industry peers.
5. An important point to note is that 23% of the respondents reported that their organizations benchmark their CMM activities with global organizations.

C. Analysis of Competency Mapping & Management in Indian Organizations

1. Organizational Approach Model (OAM) is the most widely used competency model with over 31% of the respondents reporting its usage at their workplace
2. Individualistic model (INM) is the second most used competency model with 10% of the respondents deploying the model at their workplace
3. 8% of the respondents employed Team Approach Model (TAM)
4. 6% of the respondents employed HR system approach model (HAM)
5. 4% of the respondents had HAM and OAM deployed in their organizations
6. 2% respondents employed INM and OAM in their respective organizations.
7. 6% of the respondents had all the four models (OAM, INM, TAM and HAM) deployed at their workplace.
8. 37.5% of the respondents surveyed employed standardized models in their respective organizations
9. Of the respondents 40% of the respondents from the top and senior management roles have confirmed the use of standardized models.

10. 31% of the respondents reported that no competency models were used in their organizations.
11. The most commonly deployed organizational competency management initiatives are:
    a. Competency Based Recruitment – 69.2%
    b. Competency Based Role Mapping – 38.5%
    c. Competency Based Employee Performance Management – 33.3%
    d. Competency Based Internal Job Transfers – 25.6%
12. The most popular techniques include:
    a. Work Profile System (WPS) – 38.2%
    b. Position Information Questionnaire (PIQ) – 25.5%
    c. Competency Elicitation Interview (CEI) – 12.8%
    d. Behavioural Elicitation Interview (BEI) – 7.7%
    e. Occupational Analysis Inventory (OAI) – 7.7%
    f. Multi-purpose Occupational Analysis Interview (MOSAIC) – 2.6%
    g. Critical Incident Technique (CIT) – 0.2%
    h. Common Metric Questionnaire (CMQ) – 0.2%
    i. PIQ + OAI +WPS – 21.6%
    j. PIQ + WBS – 22.9%
    k. OAI + WPS – 10%

D. Impact of Competency Mapping & Management

1. A significant 66% of the sampled population believes that there is a positive linkage between organizational CMM and its business performance.
2. The strategic capability of an organization indicates the degree of organizations ability to adapt itself to changing social and business environments. 51% of the respondents have endorsed the positive linkage of organizational CMM and its strategic capabilities. This includes over 61% of senior and top management respondents
3. Over 64% of the respondents have reported the role of CMM in enhancing employee productivity. It goes with saying that an increase in employee productivity will lead to enhanced business performance and an increase in the

strategic capability of the organization in the long run
4. Nearly 36% of respondents believe that organizational CMM activities lead to a reduction in Employee Turnover. This figure includes 44% of respondents from the senior and top management
5. 38 % of the respondents support the positive linkage between CMM and the ability of the organizations to respond to changes in its offerings to meet changes in external business environment – Agility
6. Agility, on an organizational level, refers to efficiency with which an organization can respond to change. The linkage between organizational CMM and agility was endorsed by over 55% of the senior and top management
7. 41% of the survey respondents believe that organization CMM has contributed to increased innovation within their workplaces. Innovation refers to the ability of an organization to ensure its sustenance and competitive advantage through the design and development of innovative product and services in tune with the external socio-economic environment
8. EVA is a direct financial performance measure of the creation of shareholder wealth over a period of time. A strong EVA is highly desired irrespective of the organizational demographics. A positive impact on EVA is the ultimate endorsement of the efficacy of any management initiative. 41% of the respondents believe that there is a strong positive impact of organizational CMM initiatives on its EVA. This view is strongly supported by over 66% of the top and senior management respondents
9. It can be conclusively established that the use of standardized competency models has the maximum impact on CDI.
10. The next major contributor is the timeline for deploying organizational competency mapping and management initiatives.
11. The initiatives undertaken by an organization to benchmark its CMM initiatives also has a major impact on CDI. Peer benchmarking efforts have a greater

impact on CDI.
12. Competency mapping is an integral part of organizational CMM activities. Organizations which employ competency mapping have a significantly higher EVA.
13. The type of competency models that are used also have a significant impact on the Business performance of an organization.
14. Competency mapping and management activities have a negligible impact when done in isolation – Group or Department wise. The benefits are significantly multiplied in organizations with a holistic Competency Management Framework.
15. While an organizational CMM framework is a prerequisite for realizing significant positive impact on all operational parameters, considerable ROI can be realized by initiating CM activities across multiple departments/divisions simultaneously. The organizational Competency Management Initiatives have the most positive impact on CDI.
16. Benchmarking initiatives have a positive impact on organizational EVA. Peer benchmarking initiatives has been ranked higher that Global benchmarking initiatives
17. The use of an organizational competency dictionary impacts CDI. It ensures the positive alignment and synergy among individual, group and organizational competencies.
18. The use of standardized models (Predictor Importance – 6) enhances the effectiveness of the competency mapping and management initiatives. Over 70% of the organizations surveyed employed competency models. Of these 30% of the organizations employed standard models. The models that have significant impact on CDI include:
    a. Organizational Approach Model – 46.2%
    b. Individualistic Approach Model – 15.4%
    c. HR System Approach Model – 12.8%
19. The use of competency mapping techniques positively impact CDI. 69% of the organizations employ competency mapping techniques.

7.2 Secondary Findings & Linkages

A. Linkages

1. *There exists a strong co-relation between:*
   a. Agility & Innovation
   b. Agility and EVA
   c. Business Performance and Employee Productivity
   d. Business Performance and Employee Turnover
   e. Business Performance and EVA
   f. Business Performance and Innovation
   g. Business Performance and Organizational Strategic Capabilities
   h. Deployment of Organizational Competency Management Framework and Competency Mapping techniques
   i. Employee Productivity and Employee Turnover
   j. Employee Productivity and EVA
   k. Employee Productivity and Innovation
   l. Employee Productivity and Organizational Strategic Capability
   m. Employee Turnover and Organizational Strategic Capability
   n. Global benchmarking and Innovation
   o. Global Benchmarking Initiatives and Peer Benchmarking
   p. Innovation and EVA
   q. Organizational Strategic Capability and Agility
   r. Organizational Strategic Capability and EVA
   s. Organizational Strategic Capability and Innovation
   t. Peer benchmarking and Innovation
   u. Use of Standard Competency Models and Peer Benchmarking Initiatives
   v. Peer Benchmarking Initiatives and Organizational EVA

2. *There exists a medium co-relation between:*
   a. CMM ROI Timeline and CDI
   b. Deployment of Organizational Competency

Management Framework and use of Standard Competency Models
d. Deployment of Organizational Competency Management Framework and Peer Benchmarking initiatives
e. Deployment of Organizational Competency Management Framework and use of Organizational Competency Dictionaries
f. Deployment of Organizational Competency Management Framework and CDI
g. Global benchmarking activities and Organizational EVA
h. Global Benchmarking and Peer Benchmarking initiatives
i. Global Benchmarking initiatives and CDI
j. Peer benchmarking and timeline for CMM implementation
k. Peer benchmarking initiatives and Employee Turnover
l. Peer benchmarking initiatives and Organizational Agility
m. Use of Competency Mapping Techniques and CDI
n. Use of competency mapping techniques and Organizational EVA
o. Use of Competency Models and deployment of Competency Mapping Techniques
p. Use of Competency Models and deployment of Organizational Competency Dictionaries
q. Use of competency models and organizational competency dictionaries
r. Use of Standard Competency Models and CDI
s. Use of Standard Competency Models and CMM Implementation Timeline
t. Use of Standard Competency Models and deployment of Organizational Competency Dictionaries
u. Use of Standard Competency Models and Global Benchmarking initiatives

3. *There exists a medium negative co-relation between:*
a. CMM Implementation Timeline and Organizational EVA
b. Competency Dictionary and Employee Turnover
c. Use of Competency Mapping Techniques and Global Benchmarking Initiatives

d. Use of Competency Mapping Techniques and Organizational EVA
e. Use of Competency Models and Business Performance
f. Use of Competency Models and Employee Productivity
g. Use of Competency Models and Global Benchmarking initiatives
h. Use of Competency Models and Peer Benchmarking initiatives

4. There exists negative co-relation between:
- Use of Competency Models and Global Benchmarking Efforts
- Use of Competency Models and Peer Benchmarking Efforts
- Use of Competency Mapping Techniques and Global Benchmarking efforts

B. Primary Factors

The factor analysis of the survey data has identified four primary factors that account for 83% of the total variance (Table 5.25, Chapter 5). These four factors are in line with our research hypothesis and include Organization wide Competency Management Framework, Use of Standardized Competency Models, Peer and Global benchmarking initiatives and use of Competency Mapping Techniques

7.3 A Framework for linking Company Objectives and Personal Performance

A radical approach is to link employee performance with the organizational goals through competency management. Competencies represent integrated knowledge, skills, judgment, and attributes that employees need to perform their job effectively. A defined set of competencies for each role in the business, demonstrates the kind of employee behaviors that the organization values, and which it requires to achieve its objectives. The competency definition and creation of organizational competency dictionary can effectively integrate individual and team performance and harness synergies to help sustain organizational

mission and values. The primary advantages include the following:
- Demonstrate employee expertise
- Recruit and select new staff more effectively.
- Effective performance evaluation
- Identify skill and competency gaps more efficiently.
- Provide more customized training and professional development.
- Succession Planning
- Efficient Change Management

A competency framework is a pre-requisite to effective organizational talent management. By collecting and combining competency information, one can create a standardized approach to performance that is tangible and accessible to everyone in the company. The framework outlines specifically what people need to do to be effective in their roles and it clearly establishes how their roles relate to organizational goals and success.

Competency Framework – Design Principles

A competency framework defines the knowledge, skills, and attributes (KSA) needed for people within an organization. Each individual role will have its own set of competencies needed to perform the job effectively. An in depth understanding of the business, organizational roles is essential to develop a framework. The following design approaches may be adopted:
- Use a pre-set list of common, standard competencies, and then customize it to the specific needs of the organization
- Out-source the framework development process
- Create a general organizational framework, and use it as the basis for other frameworks as needed

Developing a competency framework can take considerable effort. To make sure the framework is actually used as needed, it is important to make it relevant to the people who will be using it and will be subsequently take its ownership. The following three principles are critical when designing a competency framework:

1. Involve the people doing the work – These frameworks should not be developed solely by HR personnel (who generally are not aware of the intricacies involved in each

role), nor should they be left to line managers (who are not aware of the role fitment within the organizational structure) In order to fully understand a role one has to take inputs from the employees assigned to those roles while independently assessing the factors that differentiate successful individuals from the others

2. Communicate – People tend to get nervous about performance issues, hence the need and the objectives of the framework should be communicated to the line function. This will help in the smooth implementation of the framework

3. Use relevant competencies – Ensure that the competencies included apply to all roles covered by the framework. The listing of irrelevant competencies can have negative effect on employee performance

Competency Framework Deployment

There are four main stages in the deployment of an organizational competency mapping and management framework as illustrated in the figure.

Figure 7.1– Competency Framework Deployment

STAGE 1: ORGANIZE

1. *Defining the purpose* – The purpose for creating the framework should be clearly articulated and understood by all the stakeholders. The end objective will determine the scope and the team composition. This is an important pre-requisite prior to individual role and job analysis.
2. *Putting together a team* – The team responsible for the framework design should have representation from all the groups who would be using the framework. The team should be having focus on the long term objectives of the organization while designing the framework.

STAGE 2 – GATHER

This is the primary stage in the design and deployment of the framework. The quality of data collected will impact the accuracy of the framework.

The following are some of the recommended techniques for data collection:

- *Observation* – This technique is the best for jobs involving hand-on labour. Observing employees at the workplace can provide a lot of relevant inputs impacting the framework design.
- *Interviews* – It is advisable to employ general group as well as stratified focused group supplemented by individual interviews to gather macro and micro level details regarding individual jobs as well as group objectives.
- *Questionnaire Based Surveys* – A survey is an efficient way to gather data. However it is important that considerable effort goes into designing questions that will elicit the information pertinent to the framework design. The reliability and the validity of the questionnaire are to be determined. In some cases it might be easier to use a standardized questionnaire. However the reliability of the questionnaire on the target population needs to be verified.
- *Job Analysis* – It is very important to ensure that all the

pertinent job behaviors are included in the framework. They would typically include the following:
- Business plans, strategies, and objectives
- Organizational principles
- Job descriptions
- Regulatory or other compliance issues
- Predictions for the future of the organization or industry
- Customer and supplier requirements

Job analysis that includes a variety of techniques and considerations will give the most comprehensive and accurate results. An organizational framework mandates the presence of sample of roles from across the company. This will help capture the widest range of competencies that are still relevant to the whole business.

As information is gathered about each role it should be documented as separate behavioral statements. In stage 3 the information collected would be organized into larger competencies. It is therefore important that the raw data collected in stage 2 is analyzed and grouped effectively.

☐ STAGE 3 - CONSTRUCT

This stage involves grouping all of the behaviors and skill sets into competencies. The important steps in this stage are:

1. *Grouping the statements* – The behavior statements collected in stage 2 should be grouped to identify common skills. The goal is to have three or four groups. An example could be - manual skills, decision-making and judgment skills, and interpersonal skills.
2. *Create subgroups* – The groups would need to be broken down to into subcategories of related behaviors. Typically, there will be three or four sub groupings for each larger category. This provides the basic structure of the competency framework.
3. *Refine the subgroups* – For each of the larger categories, define the subgroups even further. It is important to analyze the inter-relationships of the behaviors and

revise the groupings as necessary.
4. *Identify and name the competencies* – The final step is to identify a specific competency to represent each of the smaller subgroups of behaviors. These competencies can be used to name the larger group category. It is a good practice to add levels for each competency. This is particularly useful when using the framework for compensation or performance reviews. This can be achieved by dividing the related behaviors of each competency into measurement scales according to complexity, responsibility, scope, or other relevant criteria. The existing job grading scales may be used for this purpose.
- The defined competencies may be validated and revised based on the following checklist:
- Is this behavior demonstrated by people who perform the work most effectively? In other words, are people who don't demonstrate this behavior ineffective in the role?
- Is this behavior relevant and necessary for effective work performance?

A survey could be used to gather information about the effectiveness of the defined competencies. It is important to look for consensus among the employees performing the job (for which the competencies are defined) as well as areas where there is little agreement. It is essential that the language or the way the competencies are described are simple to understand and more importantly to implement.

STAGE 4 - EXECUTE

Effective communication regarding the need and benefits of the developed framework is an important precursor to the framework rollout. This would help in getting the buy-in from the employees. The following is the final checklist prior to the framework deployment:
1. *Link to business objectives* – Linkages between individual competencies and organizational goals and values
2. *Reward & Recognition* – Effective Recognition & Rewards (R&R) structure

3. *Coaching & Mentoring* – Training, coaching and mentoring employees on the critical activities to support the framework
4. *Simplicity* – It is effective to start with a simple framework, gather acceptance, verify its effectiveness and incorporate learning's and experiences while dynamically updating the core

7.4 Recommendations

1. *Develop an Organizational Competency Framework*
   Defining and measuring employee performance is critical to success of business enterprises. Effective measurement is possible only if the key parameters that define employee performance at the workplace is identified and defined. These parameters include the skills, behaviors, and attitudes that employees need to perform their roles effectively. There are different techniques, methods that attempt to define a set of measures for analyzing employee performance but none of them have been able to provide a holistic evaluation.
2. *Establish Benchmarking Initiatives*
   Benchmarking is an effective exercise to establish baselines, define best practices, identify improvement opportunities and create a competitive environment within the organization. Benchmarking helps organizations gain an independent perspective about how well they perform compared to their peers, clearly identify specific areas of opportunity, validate assumptions, and prioritize improvement opportunities, set performance expectations and monitor organizational performance while managing change.
   a. Integrating benchmarking with the organization culture will result in valuable data that encourages discussion innovation and optimal practices. It is imperative that an organization benchmarks its CMM initiatives with its industry peers from the early stages of

implementation.
   b. It has been established that benchmarking increases the potency of the CMM initiatives. Once the CMM framework has been deployed, models generated and competency mapping initiatives rolled out, an organization can attempt to benchmark its initiatives with global standards and best practices.
3. *Use Standard Competency Models*
   Organizations should employ standardized competency models if they are available. The standard models may be customized at a later stage to suit the specific business requirements. In case standard models are not available, organizations should build their own models. These models should be validated through the formation of expert panels ad be benchmarked against similar peer models as well as globally. The table 7.1 presents the linkage between the use of standard competency models and their impact on various operational parameters of an organization. Only 30% of the companies involved in the survey had used standard competency models. Standard behavioural, managerial and leadership competencies can be used to build a competency model for a business enterprise. The functional or technical competencies however would need some amount of customization to suit specific organizational requirements.

Table 8.1 - Impact of Standard Competency Models on Operational Parameters

S.N	Parameter	Respondents %
1	Business Performance	31
2	Strategic Capability	28
3	Employee Productivity	28
4	Employee Turnover	16
5	Agility	27
6	Innovation	26
7	EVA	35

4. Develop Organizational Competency Dictionary

Organizational competencies are usually clustered on the basis of the underlying intent which represents deep underlying organizational motives and superficial behaviours. An intent is specific to a particular circumstance and has a higher ephemeral and surface quality than the underlying motive or disposition. Competency dictionaries include all or most of the general competencies needed to cover all job families and competencies that are core or common to all jobs within an organization. They may also include competencies that are more closely related to the knowledge and skills needed for specific jobs or functions

A competency dictionary presents the competencies in a generic form, in scales designed to cover behaviour in a wide range of jobs and needs to be adapted for a variety of applications. Competency dictionaries include all or most of the general competencies needed to cover all job families and competencies that are core or common to all jobs within an organization. These include competencies that are more closely related to the knowledge, skills and attributes (KSAs) needed for specific jobs or functions.

Only 23% of the survey respondents have reported the use of competency dictionaries. Over 30% of the total respondents believe that there is a strong linkage between the use of competency dictionaries and increased EVA. 88% of the respondents who use competency dictionaries have recorded a positive impact on EVA. Competency dictionary is a practical tool that acts as a foundation for quick and cost effective way for the implementation of talent management across the organization. A competency dictionary is critical to organizational success

Summary

Creating a competency framework is an effective method to assess, maintain, and monitor the KSA's of employees within an organization. The framework facilitates the measurement of the current competency levels to ensure that the employees have the expertise needed to add value to the business. It also helps line managers make informed decisions about talent recruitment, retention, and succession strategies. By identifying the specific behaviors and skills needed for each role, it enables an organization to budget and plan for employee learning and development. The process of creating a competency framework is long and complex. It is important to involve all the stakeholders in the entire value chain, from planning to deployment, to ensure a successful outcome. However the deployment of the Competency Mapping and Management framework is crucial to ensure the long term success of the organization. Human Resources Management (HRM) adds value (HVA – Human Capital Value Added) when it helps individuals and organizations perform better than their current levels. The organizational framework should encompass a competency dictionary; include standard competency models, CMM techniques and benchmarking initiatives. This research focused on identifying those measurable human behaviors and deployable organizational CMM initiatives that would help in predicting as well as achieving superior individual and organizational performance.

KEY TERMS

3rd Generation Partnership Project (3GPP)
3rd Generation Partnership Project 2 (3GPP2)
Air Conditioner (AC)
Automatic Cell Planning (ACP)
AVE (Average Variance Extracted)
Behavioural Elicitation Interview (BEI)
Bill of Materials (BoM)
Billing Support System (BSS)
Border Gateway Protocol (BGP)
Certified Information Systems Auditor (CISA)
Certified Information Systems Security Professional (CISSP)
Classification and Regression Tree (CART)
Code Division Multiple Access (CDMA)
Common Metric Questionnaire (CMQ)
Competency Deployment Index (CDI)
Competency Elicitation Interview (CEI)
Competency Management (CM)
Competency Mapping & Management (CMM)
Confirmatory Factor Analysis (CFA)
Critical Incident Technique (CIT)
Customer Value Proposition (CVP)
Data Communication Network (DCN)
Dense Wavelength Division Multiplexing (DWDM)
Diesel Generator (DG)
Digital Loop Carrier (DLC)
Economic Value Added (EVA)
Element Management System (EMS)
Emotional intelligence (EI)
Employee Value Proposition (EVP)
Enhanced Interior Gateway Routing Protocol (EIGRP)
European Union (EU)
Fixed Access (FA)
Fixed Wireless Access (FWA)
General Packet Radio Service (GPRS)
Global System for Mobile Communications (GSM)
High Speed Data (HSD)
HR System Approach Model (HAM)

HRVA (Human Resource Value Added)
Human Resources (HR)
Human Value Added (HVA)
Individualistic Approach Model (IAM)
Intellectual Capital (IC)
Intellectual Quotient (IQ
International Organization for Standardization (ISO)
Internet Protocol Version 4 (IP V4)
Internet Protocol Version 4 (IP V6)
ISO – Information Security Management Standard (ISO27001)
Just-in-Time (JIT)
Key Performance Indicator (KPI)
Key Result Areas (KRA)
Knowledge areas, skills, abilities, other personal attributes (KSAO)
Knowledge Management (KM)
Knowledge, Skills & Attributes (KSA)
Large Signal Polar Modulation (LSPM)
Layer 3 Virtual Private Network (L3VPN)
Local Multipoint Distribution Service (LMDS)
Long-Term Evolution (LTE)
Mean Time to Repair (MTTR)
Metro Ethernet Network (MEN)
Multi-national Corporation (MNC)
Multi-Protocol Label Switching (MPLS)
Multi-purpose Occupational Analysis Interview (MOSAIC)
Network Management System (NMS)
Next Generation Networks (NGN)
Occupational Analysis Inventory (OAI)
Open Shortest Path First (OSPF)
Operation Support System (OSS)
Operational Expenditure (OPEX)
Operations & Maintenance (OAM)
Optical Fiber Cable (OFC)
Optical Time Domain Reflectometer (OTDR)
Optical Transport Network (OTN)
Organizational Approach Model (OAM)
Partial Least Squares Regression (PLS)
Position Information Questionnaire (PIQ)
Return on Investments (ROI)

Root Cause Analysis (RCA)
Router Information Protocol (RIP)
Service Level Agreement (SLA)
Subject Matter Expert (SME)
Supply Chain Management (SCM)
Switched Mode Power Supply (SMPS)
Synchronous Digital Hierarchy (SDH)
Systems, Applications & Products in Data Processing (SAP)
Telecom Enforcement, Resource and Monitoring (TERM)
Telecom Regulatory Authority of India (TRAI)
TEMS CellPlanner Universal (TCPU)
Third Generation (3G)
Training & Development (T&D)
Training Need Analysis (TNA)
United Kingdom (UK)
United States of America (USA)
Universal Mobile Telecommunications System (UMTS)
Unspecified Bit Rate (UBR)
Very Small Aperture Terminal (VSAT)
Wireless Planning & Coordination (WPC)
Work Profile System (WPS)

REFERENCES

Ashkezar, M. J., & Aeen, M. N. (2012). Using Competency Models to Improve HRM. Ideal Type of Management, 59-68.

Avilar. (2008). Human Capital Management. Retrieved December 26, 2010, from avilar.com: www.avilar.com

Bersin & Associates (2008) Organizational Talent Management. Retrieved July 1, 2010, from www.bersin.com: www.bersin.com

Blaenau Gwent. (2009). Middle Manager Framework. Retrieved April 14, 2010, from Blaenau Gwent: http://www.blaenau-gwent.gov.uk/

Blitz, D. C. (2011, March 3). Benchmarking Benchmarks. Benchmarking Benchmarks . Rotterdam: Thesis - Erasmus University.

Boxwell, R. J. (1994). Benchmarking for Competitive Advantage. McGraw-Hill Professional Publishing.

Cerovšek, T., & Zupančič, T. (2010). FRAMEWORK FOR MODEL-BASED COMPETENCY MANAGEMENT FOR DESIGN IN PHYSICAL AND VIRTUAL WORLDS. Journal of information technology in construction , 2-4.

Chhinzer, N., & Ghatehorde, G. (2009). Challenging Relationships: HR Metrics and Organizational Financial Performance . The Journal of Business Inquiry , 37-48.

Cooper, H. (1998). Synthesizing Research: A Guide for Literature Reviews. Sage Publications.

Dragonetti, N. C., Jacobsen, K., & Roos, G. (1999). THE KNOWLEDGE TOOLBOX: A Review of the Tools Available To Measure and Manage Intangible Resources. European Management Journal.

ExploreHR. (2010). Competency Based HR Management - An Essential Tool for HR Leaders. Retrieved October 13, 2011, from www.exploreHR.org: http://www.slideshare.net/nusantara99/competency-based-hr-management

FAZLAGIÆ, A. (2007, May). Utilizing Intellectual Capital in Becnhmarking Applications - Summary & Conclusion. Retrieved Jan 1, 2008

Fernandez, J. R., & Alvarez, E. (2003). Management of Internal and External Knowledge in Research and Technology Organisations. KM Summer School 2003. Knowledege Board.

Garrett, S. (2009). Competency Mapping: What Is It and How It Can Be Done by Individuals. Retrieved May 26, 2009, from http://www.careertrainer.com: http://www.careertrainer.com

Hamel, G., & Prahalad, C. (1996). Competing for the Future. Harvard Business Review Press.

Hellered, C. (2010). Benchmarking project management maturity in two organisations. Benchmarking project management maturity in two organisations . Goteborg, Sweden: Thesis CHALMERS UNIVERSITY OF TECHNOLOGY.

Hijazeh, E. H. (2011). Adopting a Competency Based Human Resource Management System in Palestine Cellular Communication LTD-JAWWAL. Adopting a Competency Based Human Resource Management System . Nablus, Palestine: An-Najah National University.

Hunter, Schmidt and Judiesch (1990), Individual differences in output variability as a function of job Complexity, Journal of Applied Psychology, 75(1), 28-42

Investopedia . (2011, Nov). Retrieved July 01, 2011, from Investopedia: http://www.investopedia.com/terms/e/eva.asp#axzz22pniZTa8

Investopedia. (2010). Investopedia. Retrieved April 22, 2010, from Investopedia: http://www.investopedia.com/terms/v/valueproposition.asp

Jean, H. M., & Despres, C. (1994). Benchmarking HR Practices: Approaches, Rationales and Prescriptions for Action . The International Institute for Management Development , 2-20.

Kandula, S. R. (2000). Human Resource Management in Practice. Prentice Hall of India Private Limited.

Kevin, M. (2007). Competency Management: The Link between Talent Management and Optimum Business Results. Retrieved July 1, 2011, from Aberdeen Group:

http://www.aberdeen.com/Aberdeen-Library/4314/RA-competency-management.aspx

Khandwalla, P. N. (2004, October). http://www.vikalpa.com. Retrieved 12 19, 2011, from http://www.vikalpa.com: http://www.vikalpa.com/pdf/articles/2004/2004_oct_dec_10_24.pdf

Kotwal, M. (2006). Model, and Method for Competency Mapping and Assessment - Sunrise Model. Mumbai: SunRise Management Consulting Services.

Lake, L. (2010). Develop your Value Proposition. Retrieved April 22, 2010, from About.com: Lake, L. (2010). Develop your Value Proposition. Retrieved 4 22, 2010, from About.com: Marketing:http://marketing.about.com/od/marketingplanandstrategy/a/valueprop.htm

LaRocca, M. (2010, January). Career and Competency Pathing:The Competency Modeling Approach. Retrieved January 13, 2010, from http://edweb.sdsu.edu: http://edweb.sdsu.edu/people/arossett/pie/interventions/career_1.htm

Ley, T. (2006, March). Organizationa lCompetency Management - A Competence Performance Approach. Organizational Competency Management - A Competence Performance Approach . Austria: Dissertation - University of Graz.

Ley, T., & Albert, D. (2003). Identifying Employee Competencies in Dynamic Work Domains: Methodological Considerations and a Case Study. Journal of Universal Computer Science , 1500-1518.

Management Study Guide. (n.d.). Competency-Management-for-Performance-Benchmarks.htm. Retrieved December 25, 2010, from http://www.managementstudyguide.com: http://www.managementstudyguide.com/competency-management-for-performance-benchmarks.htm

Michington, B. (2006). Your Employer Brand – attract, engage, retain. Australia: Collective Learning.

Michington, B. (2010). Employer Brand Leadership - A Global Perspective. Australia: Collective Learning.

Mukherjee, S. D. (2011-12). Competency Mapping for Superior Results. Mc Graw Hill Education.

Mukhopadhyay, K., Sil, J., & Banerjea, N. (June 2011). A Competency Based Management System for Sustainable Development by Innovative Organizations. The Journal of Business Perspective Vol.15 No. 2 , 153-162.

Nevis, E. C., DiBella, A. J., & Gould, J. M. (1995, January 15). Understanding Organizations as Learning Systems. MIT Sloan Management Review.

Patricia, O. d., & Miltiadis, L. D. (2008). Competencies and human resource management: implications for organizational competitive advantage. Journal of Knowledge Management , 54.

Prasad, S. K., & Rahman, S. U. (2002). Talent Management- Leveraging Talent for Business Results.

Rao, T. (2007). Global Leadership and Managerial Competencies of Indian Managers. IIMA-India , 2-28.

Reider, R., & Reider, H. R. (2000). Benchmarking Strategies: A Tool for Profit Improvement. John Wiley & Sons Inc.

Rothwell, J. W., & Duboise, D. D. (2004). Competency-Based Human Resource Management.

Sanghvi, S. (2007). The Handbook of Competency Mapping: Understanding, Designing and Implementing Competency Models in Organizations. Amazon Createspace.

Schieltz, M. (n.d.). Competency Models. Retrieved May 25, 2010, from Chron.com: http://smallbusiness.chron.com/types-competency-models-15377.html

Shellabea, S. (2006). Competency profiling: definition and implementation. Retrieved April 5, 2010, from Consult Seven: http://www.consultseven.com/Insight/pdf/Competency_P rofiling.pdf

Spencer, L. M., & Spencer, S. M. (2008). Competence at Work. John Wiley & Sons Inc.

Strassmann, P. A. (1999, October). Calculating Knowledge Capital. Retrieved December 9, 2010, from http://www.strassmann.com: http://www.strassmann.com/pubs/km/1999-10.php

Sunrise Management Consulting Services. (2008). Model, and Method for Process Oriented Employee Performance

Appraisal. Retrieved June 13, 2008, from Sunrise Consulting: http://www.sunriseconsultinggroup.net/scg/

Survey Analytics. (n.d.). Benchmarking - Enterprise Feedback Management. Retrieved Nov 23, 2011, from Survey Analytics: http://www.surveyanalytics.com/application/surveyanalytics/products/benchmarking.html

Sveiby, K. E. (1996). Measuring Competence.

The Danish Trade and Industry Development Council. (1997). Reporting and Managing Intellectual Capital. Danish Agency for Trade and Industry.

The Economist Intelligence Unit Limited. (2009, Jan). Organisational agility:How business can survive and thrive in turbulent times. The Economist, pp. 3-28.

Tóth, E. (2012). The Role of Cross-cultural Competencies in Start-up Companies. Thesis for the Degree of Master of Science in Human Resource Management, University of Iceland.

Warier, S. (2003). Knowledge Management. Mumbai: Vikas Publishing House Pvt. Limited.

Warier, S. (2007). Measuring Organizational Intangible Assets - Human Capital. Indian Society for Training & Development.

Warier, S. (2007). Metrics for Organizational Intangible Assets Measurement. Indian Society for Training & Development.

Wikipedia. (2008). Competency Management. Retrieved July 31, 2011, from Wikipedia: http://findtalent-keeptalent.wikispaces.com/Competency+Management

Wikipedia. (2010, October). Competency dictionary. Retrieved January 13, 2011, from Wikipedia: http://en.wikipedia.org/wiki/Competency_dictionary

Workitect. (2007). Competency Dictionary. Retrieved April 14, 2008, from www.workitect.com: www.workitect.com

APPENDIX

Final Survey Questionnaire

Organizational Competency Mapping & Management

1. Demographics

This section is used only to create a demographic profile of the survey participants. The personal information entered in this section will not be shared with any outside source in any form and will not feature in the final report.

This survey is designed to garner primary data for my doctoral thesis. There are a total of 35 questions spread over 3 pages and the total time required for the survey is less than 5 minutes.

Sudhir Warier
Research Scholar - AMU - India

* 1. What is your first name?

* 2. What is your last name?

* 3. Are you male or female?
○ Male
○ Female

* 4. Are you an Indian National?
○ Yes ○ No

* 5. Which category below includes your age?
○ 17 or younger
○ 18-20
○ 21-29
○ 30-39
○ 40-49
○ 50-59
○ 60 or older

Organizational Competency Mapping & Management

*6. What is the highest level of school you have completed or the highest degree you have received?

○ Less than high school degree
○ High school degree or equivalent
○ Graduate
○ Post Graduate
○ M.Phil or Equivalent
○ Doctoral
○ Post Doctoral

*7. Which of the following categories best describes your employment status?

○ Not Employed
○ Student
○ Home Maker
○ Retired
○ Self Employed
○ Contract/Temporary Employment
○ Consultant
○ Government Service
○ Public Enterprise
○ Private Enterprise
○ Other (please specify)
[_____]

*8. If employed, Please select the industry that you are associated with
[_____]
[_____]

*9. Please select the number of employees in your organization:
[_____]

COMPETENCY MAPPING & MANAGEMENT – *A Comprehensive Survey*

Organizational Competency Mapping & Management

*10. Please provide the following demographic information

Company:
Address 1:
Address 2:
City/Town:
State/Province:
ZIP/Postal Code:
Country:
Email Address:
Phone Number:

2. Organizational Competency Management & Mapping Evaluation

*11. Does your organization employ a Competency Management Framework?

○ Yes
○ No
○ Don't Know

*12. Does your organization have plans to initiate CM activities in the near future?

○ Yes
○ No
○ N/A

*13. Does you organization employ competency models?

○ Yes
○ No
○ Not Applicable

*14. Please select the type of Competency Model used in your organization.

☐ Organizational Approach Model
☐ HR System Approach Model
☐ Team Approach Model
☐ Individualistic Models
☐ Not Applicable
☐ Don't Know
☐ Other (please specify)

Organizational Competency Mapping & Management

*15. Please choose the approriate Organizational Approach Model used in your organization.

- [ ] Normative Model (Effective Hierarchical Organizations)
- [ ] Learning Organizations
- [ ] Not Applicable
- [ ] Don't Know
- [ ] Other (please specify)

*16. Please choose the approriate HR System Approach Model used in your organization.

- ○ Contigency Model
- ○ Not Applicable
- ○ Don't Know
- ○ Other (please specify)

*17. Please choose the approriate Team Approach Model used in your organization.

- [ ] Campion's Model
- [ ] Not Applicable
- [ ] Don't Know
- [ ] Other (please specify)

*18. Please choose the approriate Individualistic Approach Model used in your organization.

- [ ] Traditional Person-Job Match Model
- [ ] Strategy Based Model
- [ ] Strategy Development Model
- [ ] Intellectual Capital Model
- [ ] Not Applicable
- [ ] Don't Know

*19. The models employed are standardized models?

	Stongly Disagree	Disagree	Neither Agree nor Disagree	Agree	Strongly Agree	N/A
Ranking	○	○	○	○	○	○

Organizational Competency Mapping & Management

*20. Organization has a well defined Competency Dictionary?
○ Yes
○ No
○ Not Applicable
○ Don't Know

*21. Organizational CM efforts are benchmarked against peer organizations?

	Strongly Disagree	Disagree	Neither Agree nor Disagree	Agree	Strongly Agree	N/A
Ranking	○	○	○	○	○	○

*22. Organizational CM efforts are benchmarked against global enterprises.

	Strongly Disagree	Disagree	Neither Agree or Disagree	Agree	Strongly Agree	N/A
Ranking	○	○	○	○	○	○

*23. Does your organization employ competency mapping techniques?
○ Yes
○ No
○ Not Applicable
○ Don't Know

*24. The following techniques are/were used in your organization for Comptetency Mapping:
☐ Critical Incident Technique
☐ Repertory Grid Analysis
☐ Behavioural Elicitation Interview
☐ Competency Elicitation Interview
☐ Position Information Questionnaire
☐ Common Metric Questionnaire (CMQ)
☐ Multipurpose Occupational System Analysis Inventory (MOSAIC)
☐ Occupational Analysis Inventory
☐ Work Profile System (WPS)
☐ Not Applicable
☐ Don't Know
☐ Other (please specify)

3. Organizational Competency Management Impact Measurement

Organizational Competency Mapping & Management

*25. Please select the Competency Management initiatives within your organization.

- [ ] Competency Based Recruitment
- [ ] Competency Based Internal Job Transfers
- [ ] Competency Based Performance Management
- [ ] Competency Based Role Mapping
- [ ] Not Applicable
- [ ] Don't Know
- [ ] Other (please specify)

*26. There is a measurable impact of Competency Management initiatives on Organizational Business Performance.

Rating	Strongly Disagree	Disagree	Neither Agree or Disagree	Agree	Strongly Agree	N/A
	○	○	○	○	○	○

*27. There is a measurable impact of Competency Management initiatives on Organizational Strategic Capability.

Rating	Strongly Disagree	Disagree	Neither Agree or Disagree	Agree	Strongly Agree	N/A
	○	○	○	○	○	○

*28. Organizational Competency Management initiatives has resulted in increased Employee Productivity Levels.

Rating	Strongly Disagree	Disagree	Neither Agree or Disagree	Agree	Strongly Agree	N/A
	○	○	○	○	○	○

*29. Organizational Competency Management initiatives has resulted in reduced Employee Turnover.

Rating	Strongly Disagree	Disagree	Neither Agree or Disagree	Agree	Strongly Agree	N/A
	○	○	○	○	○	○

*30. Competency Management has helped your organization to adapt to the rapidly changing business landscape.

Rating	Strongly Disagree	Disagree	Neither Agree or Disagree	Agree	Strongly Agree	N/A
	○	○	○	○	○	○

Organizational Competency Mapping & Management

***31. Competency Management has helped your organization bring out innovative products and services and gain first mover advantage in the market.**

	Strongly Disagree	Disagree	Neither Agree or Disagree	Agree	Strongly Agree	N/A
Rating	○	○	○	○	○	○

***32. Please select the length of time required to kickstart Competency Management initiatives in your organization.**

○ Less than 6 months
○ Between 6 months to 1 year
○ Between 1 to 3 years
○ Between 3 to 5 years
○ Greater than 5 years
○ Not Applicable

***33. Please select the length of time elapsed before measurable ROI of Competency Management initiatives in your organization.**

○ Less than 6 months
○ Between 6 months to 1 year
○ Between 1 to 3 years
○ Between 3 to 5 years
○ Greater than 5 years
○ Not Applicable

***34. Organizational Competency Management has resulted in enhanced EVA (Economic Value Added)**

	Strongly Disagree	Disagree	Neither Agree or Disagree	Agree	Strongly Agree	N/A
Rating	○	○	○	○	○	○

4. Thank You!

Thank you for participating in this survey. The survey is used to garner primary data for my Doctoral Thesis.
Sudhir Warier
Research Scholar - AMU

35. Would you like to receive a copy of the survey report?

○ Yes
○ No

Email

Pilot Survey 1 – Reliability Test

Reliability Statistics

Cronbach's Alpha	N of Items
.630	15

Pilot Survey 3 – Reliability Test

Cronbach's Alpha	Cronbach's Alpha Based on Standardized Items	N of Items
.956	.958	10

Normality Test of Survey Data

	Tests of Normality[b,c]					
	Kolmogorov-Smirnov[a]			Shapiro-Wilk		
	Statistic	df	Sig.	Statistic	df	Sig.
Q3	.375	357	.000	.630	357	.000
Q5	.330	357	.000	.740	357	.000
Q6	.316	357	.000	.676	357	.000
Q7	.350	357	.000	.799	357	.000
Q8	.262	357	.000	.785	357	.000
Q9	.228	357	.000	.827	357	.000
Q10	.236	357	.000	.917	357	.000
Q12	.355	357	.000	.635	357	.000
Q13	.427	357	.000	.595	357	.000
Q21	.366	357	.000	.681	357	.000
Q33	.277	357	.000	.841	357	.000
Q34	.327	357	.000	.719	357	.000
Q14	.450	357	.000	.566	357	.000
Q15	.402	357	.000	.616	357	.000
Q16	.354	357	.000	.720	357	.000
Q15	.532	357	.000	.333	357	.000
Q17	.357	357	.000	.730	357	.000
Q15	.495	357	.000	.479	357	.000
Q18	.312	357	.000	.763	357	.000
Q15	.495	357	.000	.479	357	.000
Q19	.242	357	.000	.872	357	.000
Q24	.378	357	.000	.629	357	.000
Q25	.236	357	.000	.781	357	.000
Q26	.495	357	.000	.479	357	.000
Q26	.402	357	.000	.616	357	.000
Q26	.450	357	.000	.566	357	.000
Q26	.378	357	.000	.629	357	.000
Q26	.427	357	.000	.595	357	.000
Q20	.233	357	.000	.779	357	.000
Q22	.249	357	.000	.834	357	.000
Q23	.201	357	.000	.854	357	.000
Q27	.415	357	.000	.619	357	.000
Q28	.339	357	.000	.671	357	.000
Q29	.351	357	.000	.616	357	.000
Q30	.276	357	.000	.803	357	.000
Q31	.313	357	.000	.781	357	.000
Q32	.245	357	.000	.766	357	.000
Q35	.278	357	.000	.694	357	.000
Q24	.532	357	.000	.333	357	.000
Q25	.532	357	.000	.333	357	.000
Q25	.532	357	.000	.333	357	.000

Q25	.475	357	.000	.525	357	.000
Q25	.518	357	.000	.028	357	.000
Q25	.532	357	.000	.333	357	.000
Q25	.428	357	.000	.593	357	.000
Q25	.449	357	.000	.568	357	.000
a. Lilliefors Significance Correction						
b. Q25 is constant. It has been omitted.						

Final Questionnaire Reliability

S.N	Construct	Variables	No. of Questions	Questions	Coding	Cron. Alpha (α)
1	Demographic Profiling	8	8	Q3, Q5, Q6, Q7, Q8, Q9, Q10, Q11	F1R, F3R, F4R, F5R, F6R, F7R, F8R	NA (Standardized Questions)
2	Status of Competency Mapping & Management in Indian Organizations	4	4	Q12, Q13, Q14, Q24	F9R, F10R, F14R, F23R	0.71
3	Competency Mapping & Management Bench Marking Efforts in Indian Organizations	3	3	Q20, Q22, Q23	F30R, F31R, F32R	0.914
4	Analysis of Competency Mapping & Management in Indian Organizations	21	10	Q15, Q16, Q17, Q18, Q19, Q21, Q25, Q26, Q33, Q34	F17R, F16R, F18R, F20R, F22R, F11R, F24R, F25R, F12R, F13R	0.71
5	Impact of Competency Mapping & Management	7	7	Q27, Q28, Q29, Q30, Q31, Q32, Q35	F33R, F34R, F35R, F36R, F37R, F38R, F39R	0.933
6	Overall	43	32			0.91

PLS of Questionnaire Data

Variation in CDI

S.N	X	Cumulative X	Y	Cumulative Y
1	21.5962	21.5961989	89.38834	89.3883429
2	7.294466	28.8906646	8.035245	97.4235876
3	6.278124	35.1687891	1.876896	99.3004839
4	3.379345	38.548134	0.465094	99.7655782
5	3.505928	42.0540624	0.148018	99.9135963
6	5.167004	47.2210665	0.029843	99.9434391
7	2.853119	50.0741854	0.018165	99.9616044
8	3.136532	53.210717	0.011153	99.9727578
9	2.951111	56.1618277	0.00651	99.9792682
10	1.481392	57.6432197	0.00903	99.9882979
11	2.494704	60.1379236	0.002791	99.9910888
12	2.631096	62.7690196	0.001834	99.9929224
13	3.340199	66.1092191	0.001308	99.9942301
14	3.422801	69.5320198	0.001209	99.9954393
15	1.312548	70.8445683	0.002077	99.9975161

INDEX

A

Advocacy/Participatory Approach · 22
Age Profile of Respondents · 38
Agility · 3, 6, 12, 32, 73, 75, 76, 88, 89, 90, 93, 94, 95, 99, 101, 106, 133, 137, 139, 140, 149
Analytical Research · 24
Analytical Tools · 42
APPENDIX · 159
Applied Fundamental Research · 24
Arthshastra · 13
Assessment Agreement · 55
Attitude · 15

B

Benchmarking · 3, 4, 11, 31, 41, 50, 68, 69, 70, 76, 77, 78, 85, 86, 87, 101, 106, 131, 138, 139, 140, 141, 147, 154, 155, 157, 158

C

Campion's Model (CAM) · 67
CDI · 57, 58, 77, 78, 109, 110, 111, 130, 131, 137, 138, 139, 140, 151, 169
Compensation · 19
Competence · 14, 108, 156, 157, 158
Competencies · 14, 15, 49, 111, 112, 115, 141, 156, 157, 158
Competency analysis · 14
Competency Development Index · 58
Competency Management · 1, 3, 4, 6, 13, 14, 15, 16, 17, 18, 19, 26, 29, 30, 31, 32, 45, 48, 49, 67, 75, 76, 77, 79, 81, 82, 83, 85, 87, 89, 93, 94, 95, 96, 97, 98, 99, 100, 101, 110, 111, 130, 134, 138, 139, 140, 141, 151, 155, 156, 158, 174
Competency Mapping & Management · i, 2, 3, 4, 5, 6, 7, 11, 31, 32, 41, 50, 53, 81, 82, 83, 86, 87, 88, 89, 92, 93, 94, 95, 97, 98, 99, 100, 101, 105, 106, 134, 135, 136, 151, 168
competency model · 1, 2, 12, 25, 30, 31, 84, 91, 114, 131, 134, 135, 148
Competency Model for Telcos · 115
Competency Models · 2, 4, 31, 67, 77, 78, 81, 82, 83, 84, 85, 86, 87, 90, 91, 100, 111, 112, 139, 140, 141, 148, 149, 154, 157
Competency-based Training & Development · 15
Conceptual Research · 24
Confirmatory Factor Analysis · 56
Construct Validity · 58
Content Validity · 54

Contingency Model (COM) · 67
Customer Value Proposition · 3, 7, 32, 99, 100, 101, 151

D

Data Analysis · 11, 41, 44, 50
Data Coding & Tabulation · 62
Data Sources · 10, 23, 36
Data Triangulation · 23
Demographic Analysis · 63
Demographic Profile · 38
Descriptive Research · 24
Descriptive Statistics · 50

E

Economic Landscape · 3, 6, 17, 25, 32, 93, 94, 101
Emotional intelligence · 14, 151
Empirical Research · 24
Employee Competency Development · 3, 7, 32, 98, 100, 101
Employee Productivity · 3, 5, 31, 71, 72, 75, 76, 87, 88, 90, 92, 93, 95, 101, 106, 139, 141, 149
Employee Turnover · 3, 5, 32, 72, 73, 75, 76, 79, 88, 91, 93, 95, 98, 106, 137, 139, 140, 149
Research Implication – 7 · 92
EVA · 2, 3, 5, 12, 13, 15, 24, 31, 74, 75, 76, 77, 80, 87, 88, 89, 90, 91, 92, 101, 106, 107, 110, 111, 131, 133, 137, 138, 139, 140, 141, 149, 151
Exploratory Analysis · 47

F

Factorial Validity · 55
Financial Leverage · 4, 7, 32, 98, 100, 101
Fundamental Research · 24

G

Gender Profile of Respondents · 38

H

HR System Approach Model (HAM) · 67
Hypothesis - 4 Dimensions · 87
Hypothesis - 5 Dimensions · 93
Hypothesis - 6 Dimensions · 95
Hypothesis - 7 Dimensions · 97
Hypothesis - 8 Dimensions · 99
Hypothesis-1 Dimensions · 81
Hypothesis-2 Dimensions · 83
Hypothesis-3 Dimensions · 86

I

Individualistic Models (INM) · 67
Initial Transformations · 44
Innovation · 3, 6, 12, 28, 32, 74, 75, 76, 88, 89, 93, 99, 101, 106, 133, 137, 139, 149
Instrument Reliability · 51
Instrument Validity · 53
Intellectual agility · 15
Intellectual Capital · 14, 67, 115, 116, 117, 118, 123, 152, 154,

158, 174
Intellectual Quotient · 15, 49, 152
Internal Reliability of Overall Questionnaire · 53

K

Key Recruitment Parameters · 49
Key Results and Findings · 11
Knowledge Management · 16, 29, 152, 157, 158, 174
knowledge management systems · 16
KSA · 14, 90, 142, 150, 152

L

Leadership Development · 19
Learning & Adaptability · 28
Learning and Development · 19
Learning Organizations (LRM) · 67

N

Normative Model (NOM) · 67

O

Organizational Approach Model (OAM) · 67
Organizational Competency Management · 17
Organizational Competency Model Deployment · 68

P

Partial Least Square Regression · 57
performance management · 13, 14, 114
Performance Management · 19
Pilot Studies · 32
Pilot Study · 45
Pilot Study 3 Analysis · 49
Pilot Survey -1 Analysis · 48
Pilot Survey 2 Analysis · 49
Pilot Testing · 46, 47
Pragmatic Approach · 22

Q

Qualitative Research · 21
Quality of Data · 44
Quality of Measurements · 44
Quantitative Research · 21

R

Recruitment & Selection · 13
Research Constructs · 32
Research Context · 1
Research Dimensions · 32
Research Hypothesis · 2, 31
Research Implication – 1 · 82
Research Implication - 10 · 98
Research Implication – 11 · 100
Research Implication - 2 · 85
Research Implication - 3 · 87
Research Implication - 4 · 90
Research Implication - 5 · 91
Research Implication – 6 · 92

Research Implication - 8 · 94
Research Implication - 9 · 96
Research Instrument Reliability &
    Validity · 42
Research Interpretations · 133
Research Limitations · 43
Research Methodology · 22
Research Objectives · 1, 30
Research Problem · 25
Research Questions · 2, 31
Respondents Academic Profile · 38
Return on Investments · 3, 32, 152

S

Sample Size Determination · 35
Sample Size Estimation · 33
Sampling Design · 10, 33
State wise Respondent
    Distribution · 37
Strategic Capability · 3, 5, 12, 31,
    71, 75, 86, 87, 88, 92, 93, 99,
    100, 106, 133, 139, 149
Strategy Based Model (SBM) · 67
Strategy Development Model
    (SDE) · 67
Subject Matter Experts · 54
Succession Planning · 19

T

Talent Management Software
    Systems · 19
Team Approach Model (TAM) · 67
Tests of Normality · 51
Top Ten HR Challenges · 28
Traditional Pearson-Job Match
    Model (PJM) · 67
Training & Development · 13
Training Need Analysis · 18

V

Validity of the Variables · 44

W

Workforce Planning · 19

ABOUT THE AUTHOR

Sudhir Warier is a Human Capability Management Coach with expertise in organizational knowledge management and a proven track record in developing and leading learning organizations. He has over 20years of experience with over 14 years in leading the Learning & Development and Human Capital Management function. He has hands-on experience in managing the entire organization Learning & Development and Human Capital Management value chain including training delivery (Corporate/Retail), academic management, curriculum development, R&D, Talent Management, Coaching and Mentoring. He has also spent over 15 years in the field of Knowledge Management (Intellectual Capital Management) engaged in research activities, developing organizational frameworks and assessing organizational competency management initiatives. He has authored nine books and published over 30 high quality research papers in international conferences and peer reviewed journals. His book titled 'Knowledge Management' is a best seller and a reference text for varied university degree and post graduate courses internationally.

BOOKS BY THE SAME AUTHOR

S.N	Name	ISBN
1	Knowledge Management	978-8125913634
2	Data Warehousing Essentials	978-1463590482
3	Data Mining Fundamentals	978-1484145463
4	Optical Communication Fundamentals	978-1482615791
5	Strategic Management	-
6	Management Theory & Practice	-
7	Competency Management – The Conceptual Framework	978-1499236972
8	A Framework for Measuring Intangible Assets	978-1502869340
9	Competency Quotient	978-1502863454

www.ingramcontent.com/pod-product-compliance
Lightning Source LLC
Chambersburg PA
CBHW071758200526
45167CB00017B/406